EASY WEDDING PLANNING

From America's Top Wedding Experts
Elizabeth & Alex Lluch

Authors of Over 3 Million Books Sold

WS Publishing Group
San Diego, California

EASY WEDDING PLANNING

Written by Elizabeth & Alex Lluch
America's Top Wedding Experts and
Authors of Over 3 Million Books Sold

Published by WS Publishing Group
San Diego, California 92119
© Copyright 2009 by WS Publishing Group

Design by:
Sarah Jang, WS Publishing Group

For inquiries:
Log on to: www.WSPublishingGroup.com
E-mail: info@WSPublishingGroup.com

Cover photo by:
Karen French
Karen French Photography
8351 Elmcrest Lane
Huntington Beach, CA 92646
(800) 734-6219
E-mail: info@karenfrenchphotography.com
www.karenfrenchphotography.com

Printed in China

ISBN 13: 978-1-934386-54-5

THE WEDDING OF

_____

AND

_____

WHO WILL BE MARRIED ON

_____

AT

_____

CONTENTS

CONTENTS

INTRODUCTION

DEAR BRIDE AND GROOM,

CONGRATULATIONS ON YOUR ENGAGEMENT! You must be very excited to have found that special person with whom you will share the rest of your life. And you must be looking forward to what will be one of the happiest days of your life—your wedding! Planning a wedding can be fun and exciting, but it can also be very stressful; that is why WS Publishing Group created *Easy Wedding Planning*.

Easy Wedding Planning contains over 100 worksheets, checklists, timelines and comparison charts to keep you organized and on top of your plans. This new edition features a beautiful new look as well as updated wedding planning information on all aspects of the wedding planning process.

Easy Wedding Planning begins with a detailed wedding planning checklist containing everything you need to do or consider when planning your wedding and the best time frame in which to accomplish each activity. Many of the items in

INTRODUCTION

---

the checklist are followed by the page number(s) where those items are explained within the book.

The checklist is followed by a comprehensive and detailed budget analysis. This section lists all the expenses that are typically incurred in a wedding, as well as the percentage of the total budget that is typically spent in each category. Next to each expense item is the page number where you can find detailed information regarding each item.

The budget analysis is followed by a detailed description of each item in the budget, including: Options, Things to Consider, Questions to Ask, Things to Beware Of, Tips to Save Money, and Price Ranges. Our clients find this format to be both informative and easy to use, and we know you will too!

Following the detailed description of each item in the budget are wedding timelines for your wedding party as well as your service providers. Use these timelines to keep everyone on schedule.

Next is a short chapter on wedding traditions, explaining the symbolic meaning and historical significance of some of the more common wedding traditions, and a list of "Do's" and "Don'ts" when planning your wedding.

We have also included a list of responsibilities for each member of your wedding party and a breakdown of who pays for what. We also provide traditional formations for the ceremony, processional, recessional and receiving line for both Jewish and Christian weddings as well as traditional seating arrangements at the reception.

Easy Wedding Planning also has descriptions and color photographs of ninety popular wedding flowers. We hope this helps you make the appropriate flower selection and coordinate your overall color scheme.

Lastly, we have included a section to help you prepare for your honeymoon. This section will help you choose your ideal destination and develop a comprehensive budget as you plan for the vacation of your dreams. Also included are detailed packing lists, information on international travel, lists of useful resources and more.

Additional organizational features include thirteen full-color dividers. These dividers are located at the beginning of each section so you can find the information you need quickly and easily. These dividers feature beautiful photographs of weddings from around the country. Refer to these photos for inspiration and ideas.

We are confident that you will enjoy planning your wedding with the help of *Easy Wedding Planning*. Also, if you know other Options, Things to Consider, Tips to Save Money, or anything else that you would like to see included in this book, please write to us at: WS Publishing Group 7290 Navajo Road, Suite 207; San Diego, California 92119. We will include your ideas and suggestions in our next printing.

We listen to brides and grooms like you—that is why WS Publishing Group has become the best-selling publisher of wedding planners!

Sincerely,

Elizabeth H. Lluch

WEDDING PLANNING CHECKLIST

THE FOLLOWING WEDDING Planning Checklist itemizes everything you need to do or consider when planning your wedding and the best time frame in which to accomplish each activity.

As you can see, many of the items are prefaced by the page number(s) where they are explained in more detail within the book. This will help you find the information you need quickly.

This checklist assumes that you have at least nine months to plan your wedding. If your wedding is in less than nine months, just start at the beginning of the list and try to catch up as quickly as you can!

Use the boxes to the left of the items to check off the activities as you accomplish them. This will enable you to see your progress and help you determine what has been done and what still needs to be done.

WEDDING PLANNING CHECKLIST

NINE MONTHS AND EARLIER

PAGE

	❑ Announce your engagement.
	❑ Select a date for your wedding.
204	❑ Hire a professional wedding consultant.
	❑ Determine the type of wedding you want: location, formality, time of day, number of guests.
37	❑ Determine budget and how expenses will be shared.
34	❑ Develop a record-keeping system for payments made.
	❑ Consolidate all guest lists: bride's, groom's, bride's family, groom's family, and organize: 1) those who must be invited 2) those who should be invited 3) those who would be nice to invite
	❑ Decide if you want to include children among guests.
39	❑ Select and reserve ceremony site.
40	❑ Select and reserve your officiant.

NINE MONTHS AND EARLIER (CONT.)

PAGE

117 ❑ Select and reserve reception site.

53-57 ❑ Select and order your bridal gown and headpiece.

❑ Determine color scheme.

76, 199 ❑ Send engagement notice with a photograph to your local newspaper.

193 ❑ Use the calendar provided to note all important activities: showers, luncheons, parties, get-togethers, etc.

❑ If ceremony or reception is at home, arrange for home or garden improvements as needed.

67 ❑ Select and book photographer.

❑ Order passport, visa, or birth certificate, if needed, for your honeymoon or marriage license.

222 ❑ Select maid of honor, best man, bridesmaids, and ushers (approximately one usher per 50 guests).

WEDDING PLANNING CHECKLIST

SIX TO NINE MONTHS BEFORE WEDDING

PAGE

266-267	❑ Select flower girl and ring bearer.
	❑ Give the Wedding Party Responsibility Cards to your wedding party. These cards are published by WS Publishing Group and are available at major book stores.
	❑ Reserve wedding night bridal suite.
	❑ Select attendants' dresses, shoes, and accessories.
120	❑ Select and book caterer, if needed.
137	❑ Select and book ceremony musicians.
139	❑ Select and book reception musicians or DJ.
57	❑ Schedule fittings and delivery dates for yourself, attendants, and flower girl.
81	❑ Select and book videographer.
151	❑ Select and book florist.

FOUR TO SIX MONTHS BEFORE WEDDING

PAGE

189   ❏   Start shopping for each other's wedding gifts.

181   ❏   Reserve rental items needed for ceremony.

       ❏   Finalize guest list.

89   ❏   Select and order wedding invitations, announcements, and other stationery such as thank-you notes, wedding programs, and seating cards.

105, 111   ❏   Address invitations or hire a calligrapher.

193   ❏   Set date, time, and location for your rehearsal dinner.

       ❏   Arrange accommodations for out-of-town guests.

       ❏   Start planning your honeymoon.

131   ❏   Select and book all miscellaneous services, i.e., gift attendant, valet parking, etc.

       ❏   Register for gifts.

58-61   ❏   Purchase shoes and accessories.

60   ❏   Begin to break in your shoes.

WEDDING PLANNING CHECKLIST

TWO TO FOUR MONTHS BEFORE WEDDING

PAGE

143	❏ Select bakery and order wedding cake.
128	❏ Order party favors.
173	❏ Select and order room decorations.
	❏ Purchase honeymoon attire and luggage.
177	❏ Select and book transportation for wedding day.
200	❏ Check blood test and marriage license requirements.
	❏ Shop for wedding rings and have them engraved.
	❏ Consider having your teeth cleaned or bleached.
202	❏ Consider writing a will and/or prenuptial agreement.
	❏ Plan activities for out-of-town guests both before and after the wedding.
191-192	❏ Purchase gifts for wedding attendants.

SIX TO EIGHT WEEKS BEFORE WEDDING

PAGE

89, 102   ❏ Mail invitations. Include accommodation choices and a map to assist guests in finding the ceremony and reception sites.

104   ❏ Maintain a record of RSVPs and all gifts received. Send thank-you notes upon receipt of gifts.

61   ❏ Determine hairstyle and makeup.

61   ❏ Schedule to have your hair, makeup, and nails done the day of the wedding.

40-44 147   ❏ Finalize shopping for wedding day accessories such as toasting glasses, ring pillow, guest book, etc.

  ❏ Set up an area or a table in your home to display gifts as you receive them.

239   ❏ Check with your local newspapers for wedding announcement requirements.

74   ❏ Have your formal bridal portrait taken.

239   ❏ Send wedding announcement and photograph to your local newspapers.

SIX TO EIGHT WEEKS BEFORE WEDDING (CONT.)

PAGE

	❑	Check requirements to change your name and address on your driver's license, social security card, insurance policies, subscriptions, bank accounts, etc.
63	❑	Select and reserve wedding attire for groom, ushers, ring bearer, and father of the bride.
42	❑	Select a guest book attendant. Decide where and when to have guests sign in.
	❑	Mail invitations to rehearsal dinner.
200	❑	Get blood test and health certificate.
200	❑	Obtain marriage license.
196	❑	Plan a luncheon or dinner with your bridesmaids. Give them their gifts at that time or at the rehearsal dinner.
210	❑	Find "something old, something new, something borrowed, something blue, and a sixpence (or shiny penny) for your shoe."
120-125	❑	Finalize your menu, beverage, and alcohol order.

TWO TO SIX WEEKS BEFORE WEDDING

PAGE

❑ Confirm ceremony details with your officiant.

❑ Arrange final fitting of bridesmaids' dresses.

❑ Have final fitting of your gown and headpiece.

151 ❑ Make final floral selections.

101, 196 ❑ Finalize rehearsal dinner plans; arrange seating and write names on place cards, if desired.

❑ Make a detailed timeline for your wedding party.

❑ Make a detailed timeline for your service providers.

❑ Confirm details with all service providers, including attire. Give them copies of your wedding timeline.

❑ Start packing for your honeymoon.

103 ❑ Finalize addressing and stamping announcements.

TWO TO SIX WEEKS BEFORE WEDDING (CONT.)

PAGE

276   ❑ Decide if you want to form a receiving line. If so, determine when and where to form the line.

   ❑ Contact guests who haven't responded.

   ❑ Pick up rings and check for fit.

69-71   ❑ Meet with photographer and confirm special photos you want taken.

81   ❑ Meet with videographer and confirm special events or people you want videotaped.

47, 137   ❑ Meet with musicians and confirm music to be played during special events such as the first dance.

104   ❑ Continue writing thank-you notes as gifts arrive.

   ❑ Remind bridesmaids and ushers of when and where to pick up their wedding attire.

61-62   ❑ Purchase the lipstick, nail polish, and any other accessories you want your bridesmaids to wear.

   ❑ Determine ceremony seating for special guests. Give a list to the ushers.

100   ❑ Plan reception room layout and seating with your reception site manager or caterer. Write names on place cards for arranged seating.

THE LAST WEEK

PAGE

    ❑ Pick up wedding attire and make sure everything fits.

    ❑ Do final guest count and notify your caterer or reception site manager.

237-239 ❑ Gather everything you will need for the rehearsal and wedding day as listed in the Wedding Party Responsibility Cards.

222   ❑ Arrange for someone to drive the getaway car.

    ❑ Review the schedule of events and last minute arrangements with your service providers. Give them each a detailed timeline.

    ❑ Confirm all honeymoon reservations and accommodations. Pick up tickets and traveler's checks.

    ❑ Finish packing your suitcases for the honeymoon.

    ❑ Familiarize yourself with guests' names. It will help during the receiving line and reception.

    ❑ Notify the post office to hold mail while you are away on your honeymoon.

THE REHEARSAL DAY

PAGE

237 ❑ Review list of things to bring to the rehearsal as listed in the Wedding Party Responsibility Cards.

❑ Put suitcases in getaway car.

❑ Give your bridesmaids the lipstick, nail polish, and accessories you want them to wear for the wedding.

222 ❑ Give best man the officiant's fee and any other checks for service providers. Instruct him to deliver these checks the day of the wedding.

❑ Arrange for someone to bring accessories such as flower basket, ring pillow, guest book and pen, toasting glasses, cake cutting knife, and napkins to the ceremony and reception.

103, 222 ❑ Arrange for someone to mail announcements the day after the wedding.

181, 222 ❑ Arrange for someone to return rental items such as tuxedos, slip, and cake pillars after the wedding.

❑ Provide each member of your wedding party with a detailed schedule of events/timelines for the wedding day.

❑ Review ceremony seating with ushers.

THE WEDDING DAY

PAGE

238   ❑   Review list of things to bring to the ceremony as listed in the Wedding Party Responsibility Cards.

             ❑   Give the groom's ring to the maid of honor.

             ❑   Give the bride's ring to the best man.

             ❑   Simply follow your detailed schedule of events.

             ❑   Relax and enjoy your wedding!

BUDGET ANALYSIS

THIS COMPREHENSIVE BUDGET ANALYSIS has been designed to provide you with all the expenses that can be incurred in any size wedding, including such hidden costs as taxes, gratuities, stamps, and other items that can easily add up to thousands of dollars in a wedding. After you have completed this budget, you will have a much better idea of what your wedding will cost. You can then prioritize and allocate your money accordingly.

This budget is divided into fifteen categories: Ceremony, Wedding Attire, Photography, Videography, Stationery, Reception, Music, Bakery, Flowers, Decorations, Transportation, Rental Items, Gifts, Parties, and Miscellaneous.

At the beginning of each category is the percentage of a total wedding budget that is typically spent in that category, based on national averages. Multiply your intended wedding budget by this percentage and write that amount in the

BUDGET ANALYSIS

"Typically" space provided.

To determine the total cost of your wedding, estimate the amount of money you will spend on each item in the budget analysis and write that amount in the "Budget" column after each item. Next to each expense item is the page number where you can find detailed information about it. Items printed in italics are traditionally paid for by the groom or his family.

Add all the "Budget" amounts within each category and write the total amount in the "Subtotal" space at the end of each category. Then add all the "Subtotal" figures to come up with your final wedding budget. The "Actual" column is for you to input your actual expenses as you purchase items or hire your service providers. Writing down the actual expenses will help you stay within your budget.

For example, if your total wedding budget is $60,000, write this amount at the top of page 28. To figure your typical ceremony expenses, multiply $60,000 by .05 (5%) to get $3,000. Write this amount on the "Typically" line in the "Ceremony" category to serve as a guide for all your ceremony expenses.

If you find, after adding up all your "Subtotals," that the total amount is more than what you had in mind to spend, simply decide which items are more important to you and adjust your expenses accordingly.

CHECKLIST OF BUDGET ITEMS

CEREMONY

- ❏ Ceremony Site Fee
- ❏ *Officiant's Fee*
- ❏ *Officiant's Gratuity*
- ❏ Guest Book/Pen/Penholder
- ❏ Ring Bearer Pillow
- ❏ Flower Girl Basket

WEDDING ATTIRE

- ❏ Bridal Gown
- ❏ Alterations
- ❏ Headpiece/Veil
- ❏ Gloves
- ❏ Jewelry
- ❏ Garter/Stockings
- ❏ Shoes
- ❏ Hairdresser
- ❏ Makeup Artist
- ❏ Manicure/Pedicure
- ❏ *Groom's Formal Wear*

PHOTOGRAPHY

- ❏ Bride & Groom's Album
- ❏ Engagement Photograph
- ❏ Formal Bridal Portrait
- ❏ Parents' Album
- ❏ Proofs/Previews
- ❏ Digital Files
- ❏ Extra Prints

VIDEOGRAPHY

- ❏ Main Video
- ❏ Titles
- ❏ Extra Hours
- ❏ Photo Montage
- ❏ Extra Copies

STATIONERY

- ❏ Invitations
- ❏ Response Cards
- ❏ Reception Cards
- ❏ Ceremony Cards
- ❏ Pew Cards
- ❏ Seating/Place Cards
- ❏ Rain Cards
- ❏ Maps
- ❏ Ceremony Programs
- ❏ Announcements
- ❏ Thank-You Notes
- ❏ Stamps
- ❏ Calligraphy
- ❏ Napkins/Matchbooks

RECEPTION

- ❏ Reception Site Fee
- ❏ Hors d'Oeuvres
- ❏ Main Meal/Caterer
- ❏ Liquor/Beverages
- ❏ Bartending/Bar Setup Fee
- ❏ Corkage Fee
- ❏ Fee to Pour Coffee

Items in italics are traditionally paid for by the groom or his family.

CHECKLIST OF BUDGET ITEMS

RECEPTION (CONT.)

- ❑ Service Providers' Meals
- ❑ Gratuity
- ❑ Party Favors
- ❑ Disposable Cameras
- ❑ Rose Petals/Rice
- ❑ Gift Attendant
- ❑ Parking Fee/Valet Services

MUSIC

- ❑ Ceremony Music
- ❑ Reception Music

BAKERY

- ❑ Wedding Cake
- ❑ *Groom's Cake*
- ❑ Cake Delivery/Setup Fee
- ❑ Cake-Cutting Fee
- ❑ Cake Top
- ❑ Cake Knife/Toasting Glasses

FLOWERS

BOUQUETS
- ❑ *Bride*
- ❑ Tossing
- ❑ Maid of Honor
- ❑ Bridesmaid

FLOWERS (CONT.)

FLORAL HAIRPIECES
- ❑ Maid of Honor/Bridesmaids
- ❑ Flower Girl

CORSAGES
- ❑ *Bride's Going Away*
- ❑ *Family Members*

BOUTONNIERES
- ❑ *Groom*
- ❑ *Ushers/Other Family Members*

CEREMONY SITE
- ❑ Main Altar
- ❑ Altar Candelabra
- ❑ Aisle Pews

RECEPTION SITE
- ❑ Head Table
- ❑ Guest Tables
- ❑ Buffet Table
- ❑ Punch Table
- ❑ Cake Table
- ❑ Cake
- ❑ Cake Knife
- ❑ Toasting Glasses
- ❑ Floral Delivery/Setup Fee

Items in italics are traditionally paid for by the groom or his family.

CHECKLIST OF BUDGET ITEMS

DECORATIONS

- ❏ Table Centerpieces
- ❏ Balloons

TRANSPORTATION

- ❏ Transportation

RENTAL ITEMS

- ❏ Bridal Slip
- ❏ Ceremony Accessories
- ❏ Tent/Canopy
- ❏ Dance Floor
- ❏ Tables/Chairs
- ❏ Linen/Tableware
- ❏ Heaters
- ❏ Lanterns
- ❏ Other Rental Items

GIFTS

- ❏ *Bride's Gift*
- ❏ Groom's Gift
- ❏ Bridesmaids' Gifts
- ❏ *Ushers' Gifts*

PARTIES

- ❏ Bridesmaids' Luncheon
- ❏ Rehearsal Dinner

MISCELLANEOUS

- ❏ Newspaper Announcements
- ❏ *Marriage License*
- ❏ *Prenuptial Agreement*
- ❏ Bridal Gown Preservation
- ❏ Bridal Bouquet Preservation
- ❏ Wedding Consultant
- ❏ Wedding Planning Online
- ❏ Taxes

Items in italics are traditionally paid for by the groom or his family.

BUDGET ANALYSIS

WEDDING BUDGET	Budget	Actual
YOUR TOTAL WEDDING BUDGET	$	$
CEREMONY (Typically = 5% of Budget)	$	$
pg. 39 Ceremony Site Fee	$	$
pg. 40 *Officiant's Fee*	$	$
pg. 41 *Officiant's Gratuity*	$	$
pg. 42 Guest Book/Pen/Penholder	$	$
pg. 42 Ring Bearer Pillow	$	$
pg. 43 Flower Girl Basket	$	$
SUBTOTAL 1	$	$

WEDDING ATTIRE	Budget	Actual
WEDDING ATTIRE (Typically = 10% of Budget)	$	$
pg. 53 Bridal Gown	$	$
pg. 57 Alterations	$	$
pg. 57 Headpiece/Veil	$	$
pg. 58 Gloves	$	$
pg. 59 Jewelry	$	$
pg. 60 Garter/Stockings	$	$
pg. 60 Shoes	$	$
pg. 61 Hairdresser	$	$
pg. 61 Makeup Artist	$	$
pg. 62 Manicure/Pedicure	$	$
pg. 63 *Groom's Formal Wear*	$	$
SUBTOTAL 2	$	$

Items in italics are traditionally paid for by the groom or his family.

WEDDING BUDGET	Budget	Actual
PHOTOGRAPHY (Typically = 9% of Budget)	$	$
pg. 67 Bride & Groom's Album	$	$
pg. 73 Engagement Photograph	$	$
pg. 74 Formal Bridal Portrait	$	$
pg. 75 Parents' Album	$	$
pg. 75 Proofs/Previews	$	$
pg. 76 Digital Files	$	$
pg. 77 Extra Prints	$	$
SUBTOTAL 3	$	$

VIDEOGRAPHY (Typically = 5% of Budget)	$	$
pg. 81 Main Video	$	$
pg. 85 Titles	$	$
pg. 85 Extra Hours	$	$
pg. 86 Photo Montage	$	$
pg. 87 Extra Copies	$	$
SUBTOTAL 4	$	$

STATIONERY (Typically = 4% of Budget)	$	$
pg. 89 Invitations	$	$
pg. 96 Response Cards	$	$
pg. 98 Reception Cards	$	$

Items in italics are traditionally paid for by the groom or his family.

BUDGET ANALYSIS

WEDGET BUDGET	Budget	Actual
STATIONERY (CONT.)		
pg. 99 Ceremony Cards	$	$
pg. 100 Pew Cards	$	$
pg. 100 Seating/Place Cards	$	$
pg. 101 Rain Cards	$	$
pg. 102 Maps	$	$
pg. 102 Ceremony Programs	$	$
pg. 103 Announcements	$	$
pg. 104 Thank-You Notes	$	$
pg. 104 Stamps	$	$
pg. 105 Calligraphy	$	$
pg. 105 Napkins/Matchbooks	$	$
SUBTOTAL 5	$	$

RECEPTION **(Typically = 35% of Budget)**	$	$
pg. 117 Reception Site Fee	$	$
pg. 119 Hors d'Oeuvres	$	$
pg. 120 Main Meal/Caterer	$	$
pg. 122 Liquor/Beverages	$	$
pg. 125 Bartending/Bar Setup Fee	$	$
pg. 125 Corkage Fee	$	$
pg. 126 Fee to Pour Coffee	$	$
pg. 126 Service Providers' Meals	$	$

Items in italics are traditionally paid for by the groom or his family.

WEDDING BUDGET	Budget	Actual
RECEPTION (CONT.)		
pg. 127 Gratuity	$	$
pg. 128 Party Favors	$	$
pg. 129 Disposable Cameras	$	$
pg. 130 Rose Petals/Rice	$	$
pg. 131 Gift Attendant	$	$
pg. 131 Parking Fee/Valet Services	$	$
SUBTOTAL 6	$	$

MUSIC (Typically = 5% of Budget)	$	$
pg. 137 Ceremony Music	$	$
pg. 139 Reception Music	$	$
SUBTOTAL 7	$	$

BAKERY (Typically = 2% of Budget)	$	$
pg. 143 Wedding Cake	$	$
pg. 145 *Groom's Cake*	$	$
pg. 145 Cake Delivery/Setup Fee	$	$
pg. 146 Cake-Cutting Fee	$	$
pg. 146 Cake Top	$	$
pg. 147 Cake Knife/Toasting Glasses	$	$
SUBTOTAL 8	$	$

Items in italics are traditionally paid for by the groom or his family.

BUDGET ANALYSIS

WEDGING BUDGET	Budget	Actual
FLOWERS (Typically = 6% of Budget)	$	$
BOUQUETS	$	$
pg. 151 *Bride*	$	$
pg. 154 Tossing	$	$
pg. 155 Maid of Honor	$	$
pg. 155 Bridesmaids	$	$
FLORAL HAIRPIECES	$	$
pg. 156 Maid of Honor/Bridesmaids	$	$
pg. 157 Flower Girl	$	$
CORSAGES	$	$
pg. 157 *Bride's Going Away*	$	$
pg. 158 *Family Members*	$	$
BOUTONNIERES	$	$
pg. 159 *Groom*	$	$
pg. 160 Ushers/Other Family Members	$	$
CEREMONY SITE	$	$
pg. 161 Main Altar	$	$
pg. 162 Altar Candelabra	$	$
pg. 162 Aisle Pews	$	$
RECEPTION SITE	$	$
pg. 163 Reception Site	$	$
pg. 164 Head Table	$	$

Items in italics are traditionally paid for by the groom or his family.

WEDDING BUDGET	Budget	Actual
FLOWERS (CONT.)		
pg. 164 Guest Tables	$	$
pg. 165 Buffet Table	$	$
pg. 166 Punch Table	$	$
pg. 166 Cake Table	$	$
pg. 167 Cake	$	$
pg. 167 Cake Knife	$	$
pg. 167 Toasting Glasses	$	$
pg. 168 Floral Delivery/Setup Fee	$	$
SUBTOTAL 9	$	$

WEDDING BUDGET	Budget	Actual
DECORATIONS **(Typically = 3% of Budget)**	$	$
pg. 173 Table Centerpieces	$	$
pg. 174 Balloons	$	$
SUBTOTAL 10	$	$

TRANSPORTATION **(Typically = 2% of Budget)**	$	$
pg. 177 Transportation	$	$
SUBTOTAL 11	$	$

Items in italics are traditionally paid for by the groom or his family.

BUDGET ANALYSIS

WEDDING BUDGET	Budget	Actual
RENTAL ITEMS (Typically = 3% of Budget)	$	$
pg. 181 Bridal Slip	$	$
pg. 182 Ceremony Accessories	$	$
pg. 184 Tent/Canopy	$	$
pg. 184 Dance Floor	$	$
pg. 185 Tables/Chairs	$	$
pg. 186 Linen/Tableware	$	$
pg. 187 Heaters	$	$
pg. 187 Lanterns	$	$
pg. 187 Other Rental Items	$	$
SUBTOTAL 12	$	$

GIFTS (Typically = 3% of Budget)	$	$
pg. 189 *Bride's Gift*	$	$
pg. 190 Groom's Gift	$	$
pg. 191 Bridesmaids' Gifts	$	$
pg. 192 *Ushers' Gifts*	$	$
SUBTOTAL 13	$	$

Items in italics are traditionally paid for by the groom or his family.

WEDDING BUDGET	Budget	Actual
PARTIES (Typically = 4% of Budget)	$	$
pg. 196 Bridesmaids' Luncheon	$	$
pg. 196 *Rehearsal Dinner*	$	$
SUBTOTAL 14	$	$

MISCELLANEOUS (Typically = 4% of Budget)		
pg. 199 Newspaper Announcements	$	$
pg. 200 *Marriage License*	$	$
pg. 202 *Prenuptial Agreement*	$	$
pg. 203 Bridal Gown Preservation	$	$
pg. 204 Bridal Bouquet Preservation	$	$
pg. 204 Wedding Consultant	$	$
pg. 206 Wedding Planning Online	$	$
pg. 206 Taxes	$	$
SUBTOTAL 15	$	$

GRAND TOTAL (Add "Budget" & "Actual" Subtotals 1-15)	$	$

Items in italics are traditionally paid for by the groom or his family.

CEREMONY

CEREMONY SITE FEE

The ceremony site fee is the fee to rent a facility for your wedding. In churches, cathedrals, chapels, temples, or synagogues, this fee may include the organist, wedding coordinator, custodian, changing rooms for the bridal party, and miscellaneous items such as kneeling cushions, aisle runner, and candelabra. Be sure to ask what the site fee includes prior to booking a facility. Throughout this book, the word church will be used to refer to the site where the ceremony will take place.

Options: Churches, cathedrals, chapels, temples, synagogues, private homes, gardens, hotels, clubs, halls, parks, museums, yachts, wineries, beaches, and hot air balloons.

Things to Consider: Your selection of a ceremony site will be influenced by the formality of your wedding, the season of the year, the number of guests expected and your religious affiliation. Make sure you ask about restrictions or guidelines regarding photography, videography, music, decorations, candles, and rice or rose petal-tossing. Consider issues such as proximity of the ceremony site to the reception site, parking availability, handicapped accessibility, and time constraints.

Tips to Save Money: Have your ceremony at the same facility as your reception to save a second rental fee. Set a realistic guest list and stick to it. Hire an experienced wedding consultant. At a church or temple, ask if there is another wedding that day and share the cost of floral decorations with that bride. Membership in a church, temple, or club can reduce rental fees. At a garden wedding, have guests stand and omit the cost of renting chairs.

Price Range: $100 - $1,000

OFFICIANT'S FEE

The officiant's fee is the fee paid to the person who performs your wedding ceremony.

Options: Priest, Clergyman, Minister, Pastor, Chaplain, Rabbi, Judge, or Justice of the Peace. Discuss with your officiant the readings you would like incorporated into your ceremony. Some popular readings are:

Beatitudes	Corinthians 13:1-13
Ecclesiastes 3:1-9	Ephesians 3:14-19; 5:1-2

Genesis 1:26-28
Hosea 2:19-21
John 4:7-16
Mark 10:6-9
Romans 12:1-2, 9-18
Tobit 8:56-58

Genesis 2:4-9, 15-24
Isaiah 61:10I
John 15:9-12, 17:22-24
Proverbs 31:10-31
Ruth 1:16-17

Things to Consider: Some officiants may not accept a fee, depending on your relationship with him/her. If a fee is refused, send a donation to the officiant's church or synagogue.

Price Range: $100 - $500

OFFICIANT'S GRATUITY

The officiant's gratuity is a discretionary amount of money given to the officiant.

Things to Consider: This amount should depend on your relationship with the officiant and the amount of time s/he has spent with you prior to the ceremony. The groom puts this fee in a sealed envelope and gives it to his best man or wedding consultant, who gives it to the officiant either before or immediately after the ceremony.

Price Range: $50 - $250

GUEST BOOK/PEN/PENHOLDER

The guest book is a formal register that your guests sign as they arrive at the ceremony or reception. It serves as a memento of who attended your wedding. This book is often placed outside the ceremony or reception site, along with an elegant pen and penholder. A guest book attendant is responsible for inviting all guests to sign in. A younger sibling or close friend who is not part of the wedding party may be well-suited for this position.

Options: There are many styles of guest books, pens, and penholders to choose from. Some books have space for your guests to write a short note to the bride and groom.

Things to Consider: Make sure you have more than one pen in case one runs out of ink. If you are planning a large ceremony (over 300 guests), consider having more than one book and pen so that your guests don't have to wait in line to sign in.

Price Range: $30 - $100

RING BEARER PILLOW

The ring bearer, usually a boy between the ages of four and eight, carries the bride and groom's rings or mock rings on a pillow. He follows the maid of honor and precedes the flower girl or bride in the processional.

Options: These pillows come in many styles and colors. You can find them at most gift shops and bridal boutiques.

Things to Consider: If the ring bearer is very young (less than 7 years), place mock rings on the pillow in place of the real rings to prevent losing them. If mock rings are used, instruct your ring bearer to put the pillow upside down during the recessional so your guests don't see them.

Tips to Save Money: Make your own ring bearer pillow by taking a small white pillow and attaching a pretty ribbon to it to hold the rings.

Price Range: $15 - $75

FLOWER GIRL BASKET

The flower girl, usually between the ages of four and eight, carries a basket filled with flowers, rose petals, or paper rose petals to scatter as she walks down the aisle. She follows the ring bearer or maid of honor and precedes the bride during the processional.

Options: Flower girl baskets come in many styles and colors. You can find them at most florists, gift shops, and bridal boutiques.

Things to Consider: Discuss any restrictions regarding rose petal, flower, or paper-tossing with your ceremony site. Select a basket which complements your guest book and ring bearer pillow. If the flower girl is very young (less than 7 years), consider giving her a small bouquet instead of a flower basket.

Tips to Save Money: Ask your florist if you can borrow a basket and attach a pretty white bow to it.

Price Range: $20 - $75

- What is the name of the ceremony site?
- What is the website and e-mail of the ceremony site?
- What is the address of the ceremony site?
- What is the name and phone number of my contact person?
- What dates and times are available?
- Do vows need to be approved?
- What is the ceremony site fee?
- What is the payment policy?
- What is the cancellation policy?
- Does the facility have liability insurance?
- What is the minimum/maximum number of guests allowed?
- What is the denomination, if any, of the facility?
- What restrictions are there with regards to religion?
- Is an officiant available? At what cost?
- Are outside officiants allowed?
- Are any musical instruments available for our use?
- If so, what is the fee?
- What music restrictions are there, if any?
- What photography restrictions are there, if any?
- What videography restrictions are there, if any?
- Are there any restrictions for rice/petal tossing?
- Are candlelight ceremonies allowed?
- What floral decorations are available/allowed?
- When is my rehearsal to be scheduled?
- Is there handicap accessibility and parking?
- How many parking spaces are available for my wedding party?

CEREMONY SITE QUESTIONNAIRE

- Where are they located?
- How many parking spaces are available for my guests?
- What rental items are necessary?
- What is the fee?

- ❏ Select Prelude 1 music. Decide who will perform it.
- ❏ Select Prelude 2 music. Decide who will perform it.

- ❏ Select Processional music. Decide who will perform it.
- ❏ Select Bride's Processional music. Decide who will perform it.

- ❏ Select Ceremony 1 music. Decide who will perform it.
- ❏ Select Ceremony 2 music. Decide who will perform it.

- ❏ Select Recessional music. Decide who will perform it.
- ❏ Select Postlude music. Decide who will perform it.

UNIQUE WEDDING IDEAS

IDEAS TO PERSONALIZE YOUR CEREMONY

Regardless of your religious affiliation, there are numerous ways in which you can personalize your wedding ceremony to add a more creative touch. If you're planning a religious ceremony at a church or temple, be sure to discuss all ideas with your officiant.

The following list incorporates some ideas to personalize your wedding ceremony.

- Invite the bride's mother to be part of the processional. Have her walk down the aisle with you and your father. (This is the traditional Jewish processional.)

- Invite the groom's parents to be part of the processional as well.

UNIQUE WEDDING IDEAS

- Ask friends and family members to perform special readings.

- Ask a friend or family member with musical talent to perform at the ceremony.

- Incorporate poetry and/or literature into your readings.

- Change places with the officiant and face your guests during the ceremony.

- Light a unity candle to symbolize your two lives joining together as one.

- Drink wine from a shared "loving" cup to symbolize bonding with each other.

- Hand a rose to each of your mothers as you pass by them during the recessional.

- Release white doves into the air after being pronounced "husband and wife."

- If the ceremony is held outside on a grassy area, have your guests toss grass or flower seeds over you instead of rice.

- Publicly express gratitude for all that your parents have done for you.

- Use a canopy to designate an altar for a non-church setting. Decorate it in ways that are symbolic or meaningful to you.

- Burn incense to give the ceremony an exotic feeling.

IDEAS TO PERSONALIZE YOUR MARRIAGE VOWS

Regardless of your religious affiliation and whether you're planning a church or outdoor ceremony, there are ways in which you can personalize your marriage vows to make them more meaningful for you. As with all your ceremony plans, be sure to discuss your ideas for marriage vows with your officiant.

The following are some ideas that you might want to consider when planning your marriage vows:

- You and your fiancé could write your own personal marriage vows and keep them secret from one another until the actual ceremony.

- Incorporate your guests and family members into your vows by acknowledging their presence at the ceremony.

- Describe what you cherish most about your partner and what you hope for your future together.

- Describe your commitment to and love for one another.

- Discuss your feelings and beliefs about marriage.

- If either of you has children from a previous marriage, mention these children in your vows and discuss your mutual love for and commitment to them.

ATTIRE

BRIDAL GOWNS COME IN A WIDE variety of styles, materials, colors, lengths, and prices. You should order your gown at least four to six months before your wedding if your gown has to be ordered and then fitted. In selecting your gown, keep in mind the time of year and formality of your wedding. It is a good idea to look at bridal magazines to compare the various styles and colors. If you see a gown you like, call boutiques in your area to see if they carry that line. Always try on a gown before ordering it.

BRIDAL GOWN

Options: Different gown styles complement different body types. Here are some tips when choosing your dress:

• **A short, heavy figure:** To look taller and slimmer, avoid knit fabrics. Use the princess or A-line style. Chiffon is the best fabric choice because it produces a floating effect and camouflages weight.

- **A short, thin figure:** A shirtwaist or natural waist style with bouffant skirt will produce a taller, more rounded figure. Chiffon, velvet, lace, and Schiffli net are probably the best fabric choices.

- **A tall, heavy figure:** Princess or A-line styles are best for slimming the figure; satin, chiffon, and lace fabrics are recommended.

- **A tall, thin figure:** Tiers or flounces will help reduce the impression of height. A shirtwaist or natural waist style with a full skirt are ideal choices. Satin and lace are the best fabrics.

The guidelines below will help you select the most appropriate gown for your wedding:

Informal wedding:
Street-length gown or suit
       Corsage or small bouquet
       No veil or train

Semiformal wedding:
Floor-length gown
       Chapel train
       Fingertip veil
       Small bouquet

Formal daytime wedding:
       Floor-length gown
       Chapel or sweep train

> Fingertip veil or hat
> Gloves
> Medium-sized bouquet

Formal evening wedding:
> Same as formal daytime except longer veil

Very formal wedding:
> Floor-length gown
> Cathedral train
> Full-length veil
> Elaborate headpiece
> Long sleeves or long arm-covering gloves
> Cascading bouquet

Things to Consider: In selecting your bridal gown, keep in mind the time of year and formality of your wedding. It is a good idea to look at bridal magazines to compare the various styles and colors. If you see a gown you like, call boutiques in your area to see if they carry that line. Always try on the gown before ordering it.

When ordering a gown, make sure you order the correct size. If you are between sizes, order the larger one. You can always have your gown tailored down to fit, but it is not always possible to have it enlarged or to lose enough weight to fit into it! Don't forget to ask when your gown will arrive, and be sure to get this in writing. The gown should arrive at least six weeks before the wedding so you can have it tailored and select the appropriate accessories to complement it.

It's a good idea to put on "evening" makeup before going to try on dresses—trying on your wedding gown with a plain face is like trying on an evening dress wearing sneakers!

Beware: Some gown manufacturers suggest ordering a size larger than needed. This requires more alterations, which may mean extra charges. It is a good idea to locate a few tailors in your area and ask for alteration pricing in advance. Many boutiques offer tailoring services, but you will often find a better price by finding an independent tailor specializing in bridal gown alterations. Also, gowns often fail to arrive on time, creating unnecessary stress for you. Be sure to order your gown with enough time to allow for delivery delays and also be sure to check the reputation of the boutique before buying.

Tips to Save Money: Consider renting a gown or buying one secondhand. Renting a gown usually costs about 40 to 60 percent of its retail price. Consider this practical option if you are not planning to preserve the gown. The disadvantage of renting, however, is that your options are more limited. Also, a rented gown usually does not fit as well as a custom tailored gown.

Ask about discontinued styles and gowns. Watch for clearances and sales, or buy your gown "off the rack." Restore or refurbish a family heirloom gown. If you have a friend, sister, or other family member who is planning a wedding, consider purchasing a gown that you could both wear. Change the veil and headpiece to personalize it.

Price Range: $500 - $10,000

ALTERATIONS

Alterations may be necessary to make your gown fit perfectly and conform smoothly to your body.

Things to Consider: Alterations usually require several fittings. Allow four to six weeks for alterations to be completed. However, do not alter your gown months before the wedding. Your weight may fluctuate during the final weeks of planning, and the gown might not fit properly. Alterations are usually not included in the cost of the gown.

You may also want to consider making some modifications to your gown such as shortening or lengthening the train, customizing the sleeves, beading and so forth. Ask your bridal boutique what they charge for the modifications you are considering.

Tips to Save Money: Consider hiring an independent tailor. Their fees are usually lower than bridal boutiques.

Price Range: $75 - $500

HEADPIECE/VEIL

The headpiece is the part of the bride's outfit to which the veil is attached.

Options for Headpieces: Bow, Garden Hat, Headband, Juliet Cap, Mantilla, Pillbox, Pouf, Snood, Tiara.

Options for Veils: Ballet, Bird Cage, Blusher, Cathedral Length, Chapel Length, Fingertip, Flyaway.

Things to Consider: The headpiece should complement but not overshadow your gown. In addition to the headpiece, you might want a veil. Veils come in different styles and lengths.

Select a length which complements the length of your train. Consider the total look you're trying to achieve with your gown, headpiece, veil, and hairstyle. If possible, schedule your hair "test appointment" the day you go veil shopping— you'll be able to see how your veil looks on your hairdo!

Tips to Save Money: Some boutiques offer a free headpiece or veil with the purchase of a gown. Make sure you ask for this before purchasing your gown.

Price Range: $60 - $500

GLOVES

Gloves add a nice touch to either short-sleeved, three-quarter length, or sleeveless gowns.

Options: Gloves come in various styles and lengths. Depending on the length of your sleeves, select gloves that reach above your elbow, just below your elbow, halfway between your wrist and elbow, or only to your wrist.

Things to Consider: You may want to consider fingerless mitts, which allow the groom to place the wedding ring on your ring finger without having to remove your glove. You should not wear gloves if your gown has long sleeves, or if you're planning a small, at-home wedding.

Price Range: $15 - $100

JEWELRY

Jewelry can beautifully accent your dress and be the perfect finishing touch.

Options: Select pieces of jewelry that can be classified as "something old, something new, something borrowed, or something blue."

Things to Consider: Brides look best with just a few pieces of jewelry—perhaps a string of pearls and earrings with a simple bracelet. Purchase complementary jewelry for your bridesmaids, to match the colors of their dresses. This will give your bridal party a coordinated look.

Price Range: $60 - $2,000

GARTER/STOCKINGS

It is customary for the bride to wear a garter just above the knee on her wedding day. After the bouquet tossing ceremony, the groom takes the garter off the bride's leg. All the single men gather on the dance floor. The groom then tosses the garter to them over his back. According to age-old tradition, whoever catches the garter is the next to be married!

Stockings should be selected with care, especially if the groom will be removing a garter from your leg at the reception. Consider having your maid of honor carry an extra pair, just in case you get a run.

Things to Consider: You will need to choose the proper music for this event. A popular and fun song to play during the garter removal ceremony is *The Stripper,* by David Rose.

Price Range: $15 - $60

SHOES

Things to Consider: Make sure you select comfortable shoes that complement your gown. Don't forget to break them in well before your wedding day. Tight shoes can make you miserable and ruin your otherwise perfect day!

Price Range: $50 - $500

HAIRDRESSER

Many brides prefer to have their hair professionally arranged with their headpiece the day of the wedding rather than trying to do it themselves.

Things to Consider: Have your professional hairdresser experiment with your hair and headpiece before your wedding day so there are no surprises. Most hairdressers will include the cost of a sample session in your package. They will try several styles on you and write down the specifics of each one so that things go quickly and smoothly on your wedding day. On the big day, you can go to the salon or have the stylist meet you at your home or dressing site. Consider having him/her arrange your bridal party's hair for a consistent look.

Tips to Save Money: Negotiate having your hair arranged free of charge or at a discount in exchange for bringing your mother, your fiancé's mother, and your bridal party to the salon.

Price Range: $50 - $200 per person

MAKEUP ARTIST

A professional makeup artist will apply makeup that should last throughout the day and will often provide you with samples for touch-ups.

Things to Consider: It's smart to go for a trial run before the day of the wedding so there are no surprises. You can either go to the salon or have the makeup artist meet you at your home or dressing site. Consider having him/her apply makeup for your mother, your fiancé's mother, and your bridesmaids for a consistent look. In selecting a makeup artist, make sure s/he has been trained in makeup for photography. It is very important to wear the proper amount of makeup for photographs.

Consider having your makeup trial right before your hairdresser trial—that way you'll see how your hair looks with your makeup on. It can make a big difference.

Tips to Save Money: Try to negotiate having your makeup applied free of charge or at a discount in exchange for bringing your mother, your fiancé's mother, and your wedding party to the salon.

Price Range: $30 - $150 per person

MANICURE/PEDICURE

As a final touch, it's nice to have a professional manicure and/or pedicure the day of your wedding.

Things to Consider: Don't forget to bring the appropriate color nail polish with you for your appointment. You can either go to the salon or have the manicurist meet you at your home or dressing site. Consider having him/her give your mother, your fiancé's mother, and your bridesmaids a manicure in the same color.

Tips to Save Money: Try to negotiate getting a manicure or pedicure free of charge or at a discount in exchange for bringing your mother, your fiancé's mother, and your wedding party to the salon.

Price Range: $15 - $75 per person

GROOM'S FORMAL WEAR

The groom should select his formal wear based on the formality of the wedding. For a semiformal or formal wedding, the groom will need a tuxedo. A tuxedo is the formal jacket worn by men on special or formal occasions. The most popular colors are black, white, and gray.

Options: Use the following guidelines to select customary attire for the groom:

Informal wedding:	Business suit
	White dress shirt and tie
Semiformal daytime:	Formal suit
	White dress shirt
	Cummerbund or vest
	Four-in-hand or bow tie
Semiformal evening:	Formal suit or dinner jacket
	Matching trousers

White shirt
Cummerbund or vest
Black bow tie
Cuff links and studs

Formal daytime:

Cutaway or stroller jacket
Waistcoat
Striped trousers
White wing-collared shirt
Striped tie
Studs and cuff links

Formal evening:

Black dinner jacket
Matching trousers
Waistcoat
White tuxedo shirt
Bow tie
Cummerbund or vest
Cuff links

Very formal daytime:

Cutaway coat
Wing-collared shirt
Ascot
Striped trousers
Cuff links
Gloves

Very formal evening:

Black tailcoat
Matching striped trousers
Bow tie
White wing-collared shirt

Waistcoat
Patent leather shoes
Studs and cuff links
Gloves

Things to Consider: In selecting your formal wear, keep in mind the formality of your wedding, the time of day, and the bride's gown. Consider darker colors for a fall or winter wedding and lighter colors for a spring or summer wedding. When selecting a place to rent your tuxedo, check the reputation of the shop. Make sure they have a wide variety of makes and styles to choose from.

Reserve tuxedos for yourself and your ushers several weeks before the wedding to insure a wide selection and to allow enough time for alterations. Plan to pick up the tuxedos a few days before the wedding to allow time for last-minute alterations in case they don't fit properly. Out-of-town men in your wedding party can be sized at any tuxedo shop. They can send their measurements to you or directly to the shop where you are going to rent your tuxedos.

Ask about the store's return policy and be sure you delegate to the appropriate person (usually your best man) the responsibility of returning all tuxedos within the time allotted. Ushers customarily pay for their own tuxedos.

Tips to Save Money: Try to negotiate getting your tuxedo for free or at a discount in exchange for having your father, your fiancé's father, and your ushers rent their tuxedos at that shop.

Price Range: $60 - $200

BRIDAL ATTIRE CHECKLIST

- ❏ Full Slip
- ❏ Garter
- ❏ Gloves
- ❏ Gown
- ❏ Handbag
- ❏ Jewelry
- ❏ Lingerie
- ❏ Panty Hose
- ❏ Petticoat or Slip
- ❏ Shoes
- ❏ Something Old
- ❏ Something New
- ❏ Something Borrowed
- ❏ Something Blue
- ❏ Stocking
- ❏ Veil/Hat

PHOTOGRAPHY

The photographs taken at your wedding are the best way to preserve your special day. Chances are you and your fiancé will look at the photos many times during your lifetime. Therefore, hiring a good photographer is one of the most important tasks in planning your wedding.

BRIDE & GROOM'S ALBUM

The bride and groom's photo album is the traditional way to preserve your special day. You and your spouse will look at the photos many times during your lifetime. Therefore, hiring a good photographer is one of the most important tasks in planning your wedding.

Options: There are a large variety of wedding albums. They vary in size, color, material, construction and price. Traditional-style albums frame each individual photo in a mat on the page. Digitally designed "Montage" albums group the photos in a creatively designed fashion for a more

PHOTOGRAPHY

modern look. Find one that you like and will feel proud of showing to your friends and family. Some of the most popular manufacturers of wedding albums are Art Leather, Leather Craftsman, Capri and Renaissance. Keep in mind however, that the quality of the original photographs will determine how the finished album looks so choose your photographer for their skills, not necessarily the manufacturer of the album.

Make sure you are shown the different styles of album available. Different papers are available to print your photos, pearl and metallic as well as black and white can be chosen. Ask to see samples.

Things To Consider: Make sure you hire a photographer who specializes in weddings. Your photographer should be experienced in wedding procedures and familiar with your ceremony and reception sites. This will allow him/her to anticipate your next move and be in the proper place at the right time to capture all the special moments. Personal rapport is extremely important. The photographer may be an expert, but if you don't feel comfortable or at ease with him or her, your photography will reflect this. Comfort and compatibility with your photographer can make or break your wedding day and your photographs!

Look at his/her work. See if the photographer captured the excitement and emotion of the bridal couple. Also, remember that the wedding album should unfold like a story book -- the story of your wedding. Be sure to discuss with your photographer the photos you want so that there is no misunderstanding. A good wedding photographer will plan the day with you to ensure that all the important moments are covered. It is acceptable to take a list of important photos to your planning session before the wedding (even one copied from a wedding planning book). This will keep you on track and ensure that you've asked about all the photos that are "must haves."

Check off all photographs you would like taken throughout your wedding day.

PRE-CEREMONY PHOTOGRAPHS
- ❑ Bride leaving her house
- ❑ Wedding rings with the invitation
- ❑ Bride getting dressed for the ceremony
- ❑ Bride looking at her bridal bouquet
- ❑ Maid of honor putting garter on bride's leg
- ❑ Bride by herself
- ❑ Bride with her mother
- ❑ Bride with her father
- ❑ Bride with mother and father
- ❑ Bride with her entire family and/or any combination thereof
- ❑ Bride with her maid of honor
- ❑ Bride with her bridesmaids
- ❑ Bride with the flower girl and/or ring bearer
- ❑ Bride's mother putting on her corsage
- ❑ Groom leaving his house
- ❑ Groom putting on his boutonniere
- ❑ Groom with his mother
- ❑ Groom with his father
- ❑ Groom with mother and father
- ❑ Groom with his entire family and/or any combination thereof
- ❑ Groom with his best man

PHOTOGRAPHY

- ❏ Groom with his ushers
- ❏ Groom shaking hands with his best man while looking at his watch
- ❏ Groom with the bride's father
- ❏ Bride and her father getting out of the limousine
- ❏ Special members of the family being seated
- ❏ Groom waiting for the bride before the processional
- ❏ Bride and her father just before the processional

CEREMONY PHOTOGRAPHS
- ❏ The processional
- ❏ Bride and groom saying their vows
- ❏ Bride and groom exchanging rings
- ❏ Groom kissing the bride at the altar
- ❏ The recessional

POST-CEREMONY PHOTOGRAPHS
- ❏ Bride and groom
- ❏ Newlyweds with both of their families
- ❏ Newlyweds with the entire wedding party
- ❏ Bride and groom signing the marriage certificate
- ❏ Flowers and other decorations

RECEPTION PHOTOGRAPHS
- ❏ Entrance of newlyweds and wedding party into the reception site
- ❏ Receiving line
- ❏ Guests signing the guest book
- ❏ Toasts
- ❏ First dance
- ❏ Bride and her father dancing
- ❏ Groom and his mother dancing
- ❏ Bride dancing with groom's father
- ❏ Groom dancing with bride's mother

- ❑ Wedding party and guests dancing
- ❑ Cake table
- ❑ Cake-cutting ceremony
- ❑ Couple feeding each other cake
- ❑ Buffet table and its decoration
- ❑ Bouquet-tossing ceremony
- ❑ Garter-tossing ceremony
- ❑ Musicians
- ❑ The wedding party table
- ❑ The family tables
- ❑ Candid shots of your guests
- ❑ Bride and groom saying good-bye to their parents
- ❑ Bride and groom looking back, waving good-bye in the getaway car

Ask to look at albums that the photographer has ready to be delivered, or proofs of weddings recently photographed. Study the photographer's style. It's fine if they tell you that they're skilled in "photojournalistic" or "candid" photography but, if that's so, you should see plenty of candid-style shots in their portfolio! Some photographers are known for formal poses, while others specialize in more candid, creative shots. Some can do both.

When asked to provide references, photographers will obviously give you names of clients that they know are pleased with their work. (Why give a name of someone who wasn't?) So keep this in mind if you decide to call a former client.

When comparing prices, compare the quantity and size of the photographs in your album and the type of album that each photographer will use. Ask how many photos will be taken on average at a wedding of your size. Some photographers do not work with proofs. Rather, they simply supply you with a finished album after the wedding. Doing this may reduce the cost of your album but will also reduce your selection of photographs. Many photographers will put your proofs on a DVD for viewing. This is much less bulky and an easy way to preview all of your wedding photos.

Beware: Make sure the photographer you interview is the specific person that will photograph your wedding. Many companies have more than one photographer. The more professional companies will make sure that you meet with (and view the work of) THE photographer that will photograph your wedding. This way you can get an idea of his/her style and personality and begin to establish a rapport with YOUR photographer. Your chosen photographers name should go on your contract!

Also, some churches do not allow photographs to be shot during the ceremony. Please find out the rules and present them to your photographer so he is knowledgeable about your site.

Tips to Save Money: Consider hiring a professional photographer for the formal shots of your ceremony only. You can then place disposable cameras on each table at the reception and let your guests take candid shots. This will save you a considerable amount of money in photography.

You can also lower the price of your album by paying for the photographs and then putting them into the album yourself.

This is a very time-consuming task, so your photographer may reduce the price of his/her package if you opt to do this. To really save money, select a photographer who charges a flat fee to shoot the wedding and allows you to purchase the film.

Compare at least three photographers for quality, value, and price. Photographers who shoot weddings "on the side" are usually less expensive, but the quality of their photographs may not be as good.

Select less 8 x 10s for your album and more 4 x 6s, and choose a moderately priced album. Ask for specials and package deals.

Price Range: $900 - $9,000

ENGAGEMENT PHOTOGRAPH

The engagement photograph can be sent to your local news-papers, along with information announcing your engage-ment to the public. This announcement is usually made by the bride's parents or her immediate family. More small-town papers do this currently. The larger city papers have mostly ceased to publish engagement announcements.

Things to Consider: The photograph (usually in black and white) was traditionally of the bride alone, but today is usually of the engaged couple. The engagement portrait(s) can also be used to create a guestbook full of photos with room for guests to sign or can be framed with a wide mat to sign.

Tips to Save Money: Look at engagement photographs in your local newspaper. Then have a friend or family member take a photo of you and your fiancé in a pose and with a backdrop similar to the ones you have seen.

Price Range: $75 - $300

FORMAL BRIDAL PORTRAIT

Only a few newspapers still accept a photograph of the Bride for insertion in the newspaper the day after your wedding. For the ones that do, you'll need a studio Bridal portrait done a few weeks before the wedding so the photo can be ready. This photo, along with the announcement should be sent to the paper well ahead of time.

Things to Consider: Some fine bridal salons provide an attractive background where the bride may arrange to have her formal bridal photograph taken after the final fitting of her gown. This will save you the hassle of bringing your gown and headpiece to the photographer's studio and dressing up once again.

Tips to Save Money: If you don't mind announcing your marriage several weeks after the wedding, consider having your formal portrait taken the day of your wedding. This will save you the studio costs and the hassle of getting dressed for the photo. The photograph will be more natural since the bridal bouquet will be the one you carry down the aisle. Also, brides are always most beautiful on their wedding day!

Price Range: $75 - $300

PARENTS' ALBUM

The parents' album is a smaller version of the bride and groom's album. It usually contains about twenty 5" x 7" photographs. Photos should be carefully selected for each individual family. If given as a gift, the album can be personalized with the bride and groom's names and date of their wedding on the front cover. Small "Coffee Table" books can also be created from digital files that are montaged onto the pages. Ask to see samples of different types of parent albums available.

Tips to Save Money: Try to negotiate at least one free parents' album with the purchase of the bride and groom's album.

Price Range: $100 - $600

PROOFS/PREVIEWS

Proofs/previews or Proof DVDs are the preliminary prints or digital images from which the bride and groom select photographs for their album and for their parents' albums.

The prints vary from 4x5" to 5x5" and 4x6". The DVD allows you to view your photos on a screen in a larger size and more detail.

Things to Consider: When selecting a package, ask how many photos the photographer will take. The more images, the wider the selection you will have to choose from. For a wide selection, the photographer must take at least 3 to 5 times the number of prints that will go into your album.

Ask the photographer how soon after the wedding you will get your proofs. Request this in writing. Ideally, the proofs will be ready by the time you get back from your honeymoon.

Tips to Save Money: Ask your photographer to use your proofs as part of your album package to save developing costs.

Price Range: $100 - $600

DIGITAL FILES

Most digital files are presented as "Jpegs," which is the file type that most labs use to make prints. Your photographer will probably shoot with a professional digital camera that can create extra-large file sizes, which is important for clarity, if you want very large prints made (such as 24x30" and larger).

Things to Consider: Most photographers will not sell you the digital files up front since they hope to make a profit on selling extra prints after the wedding. Ask the photographers you interview how long they keep the files and at what point they will become available to you. A professional photographer should keep a backup copy of the digital files for at least 10 years.

Many photographers will sell you the entire set of digital files after all photos have been ordered by family and friends. Often the price will vary, depending on the amount spent on re-orders. Once you own your digital files, make a back-up copy of your disk every 5 or 6 years, as CDs and DVDs can deteriorate after 8 years or so.

Tips to Save Money: If you can wait, consider contacting the photographer a few years later and ask if s/he will sell you the negatives or files at that time. Most photographers will be glad to sell them at a bargain price.

Price Range: $100 - $800

EXTRA PRINTS

Extra prints are photographs ordered in addition to the main album or parents' albums. These are usually purchased as gifts for the bridal party, close friends and family members.

Things to Consider: It is important to discuss the cost of extra prints with your photographer since prices vary considerably. Knowing what extra prints will cost ahead of time will help you know if the photographer is truly within your budget. Think how many extra prints you would like to order and figure this into your budget before selecting a photographer.

Tips to Save Money: If you can wait, consider not ordering any reprints during the first few years after the wedding. A few years later, contact the photographer and ask if s/he will sell you the negatives/files. Most photographers will be glad to sell them at a bargain price at a later date. You can then make as many prints as you wish for a fraction of the cost.

Price Range: (5 x 7) = $5 - $20; (8 x 10) = $15 - $30; (11 x 14) = $30 - $100

*Be sure to get the photographers' business card with
name, address, phone number and email address.*

- How many years of experience do you have as a photographer?
- What percentage of your business is dedicated to weddings?
- Approximately how many weddings have you photographed?
- Are you the person who will photograph my wedding?
- Will you bring an assistant with you to my wedding?
- How do you typically dress for weddings?
- Do you have a professional studio?
- What type of equipment do you use?
- Do you bring backup equipment with you to weddings?
- Do you need to visit the ceremony and reception sites prior to the wedding?
- Do you have liability insurance?
- Are you skilled in diffused lighting & soft focus?
- Can you take studio portraits?
- Can you retouch my images?
- Can digital files be purchased? If so, what is the cost?
- What is the cost of the package I am interested in?
- What is your payment policy?
- What is your cancellation policy?
- Do you use paper proofs or DVD proofing?

- How many photographs will I have to choose from?
- When will I get my proofs?
- When will I get my album?
- What is the cost of an engagement portrait?
- What is the cost of a formal bridal portrait?
- What is the cost of a parent album?
- What is the cost of a 5" x 7" reprint?
- What is the cost of an 8" x 10" reprint?
- What is the cost of an 11" x 14" reprint?
- What is the cost per additional hour of shooting at the wedding?

VIDEOGRAPHY

NEXT TO YOUR PHOTO ALBUM, videography is the best way to preserve your wedding memories. Unlike photographs, videography captures the mood of the wedding day in motion and sound. Getting a wedding on video used to mean bright lights, cables, microphones and huge obtrusive cameras. But technology has changed, and today's videographers have more advanced equipment that allows them to film ceremonies with minimal disruption.

Today's wedding videos can also be edited and professionally produced, with music, slow motion, black and white scenes and many other special features. You have the option of selecting one, two, or three cameras to record your wedding. The more cameras used, the more action your videographer can capture—and the more expensive the service. An experienced videographer, however, can do a good job with just one camera.

VIDEOGRAPHY

OPTIONS

There are two basic types of wedding video production: documentary and cinematic. The documentary type production records your wedding day as it happened, in real time. Very little editing or embellishment is involved. These types of videos are normally less expensive and can be delivered within days after the wedding.

The cinematic type production is more reminiscent of a movie. Although it can be shot with one camera, most good cinematic wedding videos are shot with two cameras, allowing one videographer to focus on the events as they happen while the other gathers footage that will be added later to enhance the final result. This type of video requires more time due to the extensive editing of the footage, which can take up to 40 hours of studio time.

You may wish to have both of these—one straightforward version and another version with all the details and a nice, theatrical flow.

The latest technology includes the option of producing video in high definition. More televisions are being manufactured with high definition resolution, which delivers a much sharper picture than traditional sets. In years to come, viewers will encounter problems watching regular DVDs on their hi-def television sets. Standard definition video appears fuzzy and pixilated on the new high definition monitors. Having your ceremony shot in high definition will ensure that you'll be able to enjoy watching your wedding video in a crisp, clear resolution for years to come.

MAIN VIDEO

You will need to choose the type of video you want. Do you want the footage edited down to a 30-minute film, or do you want an "as it happened" replay? Remember, an edited video will require more time and will therefore be more expensive than just a documentary of the events.

Things to Consider: Be sure to hire a videographer who specializes in weddings and ask to see samples of his or her work. Weddings are very specialized events. A $1,000 video camera in the hands of a seasoned professional "wedding" videographer will produce far better results than a $3,000 broadcast quality camera or a $4,000 high definition camera in the hands of just an average camera operator. When considering a particular videographer, look at previous weddings the videographer has done. Notice the color and brightness of the screen, as well as the quality of sound. This will indicate the quality of his/her equipment. Note whether the picture is smooth or jerky. This will indicate the videographer's skill level. Ask about special effects such as titles, dissolve, and multiple screens. Find out what's included in the cost of your package so that there are no surprises at the end!

If you will be getting married in a church, find out the church's policies regarding videography. Some churches might require the videographer to film the ceremony from a specific distance.

Beware: As in photography, there are many companies with more than one videographer. These companies may use the work of their best videographer to sell their packages and then send a less experienced videographer to the wedding. Again, don't get caught in this trap! Be sure to interview the videographer who will shoot your wedding so you can get a good idea of his/her style and personality. Ask to see his/her own work.

Tips to Save Money: Compare videographers' quality, value, and price. There is a wide range, and the most expensive is not necessarily the best. The videographer who uses one camera (instead of multiple cameras) is usually the most cost effective and may be all you need.

Consider hiring a company that offers both videography and photography. You might save money by combining the two services.

Ask a family member or close friend to videotape your wedding. However, realize that without professional equipment and expertise, the final product may not be quite as polished.

Price Range: $600 - $4,000

TITLES

Titles and subtitles can be edited into your video before or after the filming. Titles are important since twenty years from now you might not remember the exact time of your wedding or the names of your bridal party members. Some videographers charge more for titling. Make sure you discuss this with your videographer and get in writing exactly what titles will be included.

Options: Titles can include the date, time, and location of the wedding, the bride and groom's names, and the names of special members of the family and bridal party. Titles may also include special thanks to those who helped with the wedding. You can then send these people copies of your video, which would be a very appropriate and inexpensive gift!

Tips to Save Money: Consider asking for limited titles, such as only the names of the bride and groom and the date and time of the wedding.

Price Range: $50 - $300

EXTRA HOURS

Find out how much your videographer would charge to stay longer than the contracted time. Do this in case your reception lasts longer than expected. Don't forget to get this fee in writing.

Tips to Save Money: To avoid paying for hours beyond what's included in your selected package, calculate the maximum number of hours you think you'll need and negotiate that number of hours into your package price.

To reduce the amount of time you'll need to use the videographer, consider recording the ceremony only.

Price Range: $35 - $150 per hour

PHOTO MONTAGE

A photo montage is a series of photographs set to music on video. The number of photographs in your photo montage depends on the length of the songs and the amount of time allotted for each photograph. A typical song usually allows for thirty to forty photographs. Photo montages are a great way to display and reproduce your photographs. Copies of this video can be made for considerably less than the cost of reproducing photos.

Options: Your photo montage can include photos of you and your fiancé growing up in addition to shots from your rehearsal, wedding day, honeymoon, or any combination thereof.

Things to Consider: Send copies of your photo montage video to close friends and family members as mementos of your wedding.

Tips to Save Money: There are many websites on the Internet that allow you to create your own photo montage either for free or at a very low price. You can then transfer your photo montage to a DVD.

Price Range: $60 - $300

EXTRA COPIES

A videographer can produce higher quality copies than you can. Ask your videographer what the charge is for extra copies.

Tips to Save Money: If you have a digital video recorder, you can make copies of your wedding video using a second DVD player. It's easier, however, to burn DVDs on your computer. Before making your own copies of your wedding video, be sure to ask your videographer if that is acceptable. Many contracts prohibit it, and doing so could be copyright infringement. Further, your videographer may have put a security device on the DVD that would prevent you from being able to copy it.

Price Range: $15 - $50

VIDEOGRAPHY QUESTIONNAIRE

- What is the name and phone number of the videographer?
- What is the website and e-mail address of the videographer?
- What is the address of the videographer?
- How many years of experience do you have as a videographer?
- Approximately how many weddings have you videotaped?
- Are you the person who will videotape my wedding?
- Will you bring an assistant with you to my wedding?
- What type of equipment do you use?
- Do you have a wireless microphone?
- Do you bring backup equipment with you?
- Do you visit the ceremony and reception sites before the wedding?
- Do you edit the tape after the event?
- Who keeps the raw footage and for how long?
- When will I receive the final product?
- What is the cost of the desired package?
- What does it include?
- Can you make a photo montage?
- If so, what is your price?
- What is your payment policy?
- What is your cancellation policy?

STATIONERY

BEGIN CREATING YOUR guest list as soon as possible. Ask your parents and the groom's parents for a list of people they would like to invite. You and your fiancé should make your own lists. Make certain that all names are spelled correctly and that all addresses are current. Determine if you wish to include children; if so, add their names to your list. All children over the age of 16 should receive their own invitation.

INVITATIONS

Order your invitations at least four months before the wedding. Allow an additional month for engraved invitations. Invitations are traditionally issued by the bride's parents; but if the groom's parents are assuming some of the wedding expenses, the invitations should be in their names also. Mail all invitations at the same time, six to eight weeks before the wedding.

STATIONERY

Options: There are three types of invitations: traditional/ formal, contemporary, and informal. The traditional/formal wedding invitation is white, soft cream, or ivory with raised black lettering. The printing is done on the top page of a double sheet of thick quality paper; the inside is left blank. The contemporary invitation is typically an individualized presentation that makes a statement about the bride and groom. Informal invitations are often printed on the front of a single, heavyweight card and may be handwritten or preprinted.

There are three types of printing: engraved, thermography, and offset printing. Engraving is the most expensive, traditional, and formal type of printing. It also takes the longest to complete. In engraved printing, stationery is pressed onto a copper plate, which makes the letters rise slightly from the page. Thermography is a process that fuses powder and ink to create a raised letter. This takes less time than engraving and is less expensive because copper plates do not have to be engraved. Offset printing, the least expensive, is the quickest to produce and offers a variety of styles and colors. It is also the least formal.

Things to Consider: If all your guests are to be invited to both the ceremony and the reception, a combined invitation may be sent without separate enclosure cards. Order one invitation for each married or cohabiting couple that you plan to invite. The officiant and his/her spouse, as well as your attendants, should receive an invitation.

Order approximately 20 percent more stationery than your actual count. Allow a minimum of two weeks to address and mail the invitations, longer if using a calligrapher or if your guest list is very large. You may also want to consider ordering invitations to the rehearsal dinner, as these should be in the same style as the wedding invitation.

SAMPLES OF TRADITIONAL/FORMAL INVITATIONS

1) When the bride's parents sponsor the wedding:

Mr. and Mrs. Alexander Waterman Smith
request the honor of your presence
at the marriage of their daughter
Carol Ann
to
Mr. William James Clark
on Saturday, the fifth of August
two thousand eight
at two o'clock in the afternoon
Saint James by-the-Sea
La Jolla, California

2) When the groom's parents sponsor the wedding:

Mr. and Mrs. Michael Burdell Clark
request the honor of your presence
at the marriage of
Miss Carol Ann Smith
to their son
Mr. William James Clark

3) When both the bride and groom's parents sponsor the wedding:

Mr. and Mrs. Alexander Waterman Smith
and
Mr. and Mrs. Michael Burdell Clark
request the honor of your presence
at the marriage of their children
Miss Carol Ann Smith
to
Mr. William James Clark

OR

Mr. and Mrs. Alexander Waterman Smith
request the honor of your presence
at the marriage of their daughter
Carol Ann Smith
to
William James Clark
son of Mr. and Mrs. Michael Burdell Clark

4) When the bride and groom sponsor their own wedding:

The honor of your presence is requested
at the marriage of
Miss Carol Ann Smith
and
Mr. William James Clark

OR

Miss Carol Ann Smith
and
Mr. William James Clark
request the honor of your presence
at their marriage

5) With divorced or deceased parents:

a) When the bride's mother is sponsoring the
   wedding and is not remarried:

Mrs. Julie Hurden Smith
requests the honor of your presence
at the marriage of her daughter
Carol Ann

b) When the bride's mother is sponsoring the
   wedding and has remarried:

Mrs. Julie Hurden Booker
requests the honor of your presence
at the marriage of her daughter
Carol Ann Smith

OR

Mr. and Mrs. John Thomas Booker
request the honor of your presence
at the marriage of Mrs. Booker's daughter
Carol Ann Smith

c) When the bride's father is sponsoring the wedding and has not remarried:

> *Mr. Alexander Waterman Smith*
> *requests the honor of your presence*
> *at the marriage of his daughter*
> *Carol Ann*

d) When the bride's father is sponsoring the wedding and has remarried:

> *Mr. and Mrs. Alexander Waterman Smith*
> *request the honor of your presence*
> *at the marriage of Mr. Smith's daughter*
> *Carol Ann*

6) With deceased parents:

a) When a close friend or relative sponsors the wedding:

> *Mr. and Mrs. Brandt Elliott Lawson*
> *request the honor of your presence*
> *at the marriage of their granddaughter*
> *Carol Ann Smith*

7) In military ceremonies, the rank determines the placement of names:

a) Any title lower than sergeant should be omitted. Only the branch of service should be included under that person's name:

Mr. and Mrs. Alexander Waterman Smith
request the honor of your presence
at the marriage of their daughter
Carol Ann
to
William James Clark
United States Army

b) Junior officers' titles are placed below their names and are followed by their branch of service:

Mr. and Mrs. Alexander Waterman Smith
request the honor of your presence
at the marriage of their daughter
Carol Ann
to
William James Clark
First Lieutenant, United States Army

c) If the rank is higher than lieutenant, titles are placed before names, and the branch of service is placed on the following line:

Mr. and Mrs. Alexander Waterman Smith
request the honor of your presence
at the marriage of their daughter
Carol Ann
to
Captain William James Clark
United States Navy

SAMPLE OF A LESS FORMAL/MORE CONTEMPORARY INVITATION

Mr. and Mrs. Alexander Waterman Smith
would like you to
join with their daughter
Carol Ann
and
William James Clark
in the celebration of their marriage

For additional wording suggestions, log on to
www.WeddingSolutions.com

Tips to Save Money: Thermography looks like engraving and is one-third the cost. Choose paper stock that is reasonable and yet achieves your overall look. Select invitations that can be mailed using just one stamp. Order at least 25 extra invitations in case you soil some or add people to your list. To reorder this small number of invitations later would cost nearly three times the amount you'll spend up front.

Price Range: $0.75 - $6 per invitation

RESPONSE CARDS

Response cards are enclosed with the invitation to determine the number of people who will be attending your wedding. They are the smallest card size accepted by the postal service and should be printed in the same style as the invitation. An invitation to only the wedding ceremony does not usually include a request for a reply. However, response cards should be used when it is necessary to have an exact head count for special seating arrangements. Response cards are widely accepted today. If included, these cards should be easy for your guests to understand and use. Include a self-addressed and stamped return envelope to make it easy for your guests to return the response cards.

Things to Consider: You should not include a line that reads "number of persons" on your response cards because only those whose names appear on the inner and outer envelopes are invited. Each couple, each single person, and all children over the age of 16 should receive their own invitation. Indicate on the inner envelope if they may bring an escort or guest. The omitting of children's names from the inner envelope infers that the children are not invited.

Samples of wording for response cards:

M_____

(The M may be eliminated from the line, especially if many Drs. are invited)

___ *accepts*

___ *regrets*

Saturday the fifth of July

Oceanside Country Club

OR

The favor of your reply is requested

> *by the twenty-second of May*
> M_____
>   *will* _____ *attend*

Price Range: **$0.40 - $1 each**

RECEPTION CARDS

If the guest list for the ceremony is larger than that for the reception, a separate card with the date, time and location for the reception should be enclosed with the ceremony invitation for those guests also invited to the reception. Reception cards should be placed in front of the invitation, facing the back flap and the person inserting them. They should be printed on the same quality paper and in the same style as the invitation itself.

Sample of a formally worded reception card:

> *Mr. and Mrs. Alexander Waterman Smith*
> *request the pleasure of your company*
> *Saturday, the third of July*
> *at three o'clock*
> *Oceanside Country Club*
> *2020 Waterview Lane*
> *Oceanside, California*

Sample of a less formal reception card:

> *Reception immediately following the ceremony*

Oceanside Country Club
2020 Waterview Lane
Oceanside, California

Things to Consider: You may also include a reception card in all your invitations if the reception is to be held at a different site than the ceremony.

Tips to Save Money: If all people invited to the ceremony are also invited to the reception, include the reception information on the invitation and eliminate the reception card. This will save printing and postage costs.

Price Range: $0.40 - $1 each

CEREMONY CARDS

If the guest list for the reception is larger than the guest list for the ceremony, a special insertion card with the date, time, and location for the ceremony should be enclosed with the reception invitation for those guests also invited to the ceremony.

Ceremony cards should be placed in front of the invitation, facing the back flap and the person inserting them. They should be printed on the same quality paper and in the same style as the invitation itself.

Price Range: $0.40 - $1 each

PEW CARDS

Pew cards may be used to let special guests and family members know they are to be seated in the reserved section on either the bride's side or the groom's side. These are most typically seen in large, formal ceremonies. Guests should take this card to the ceremony and show it to the ushers, who should then escort them to their seats.

Options: Pew cards may indicate a specific pew number if specific seats are assigned, or may read "Within the Ribbon" if certain pews are reserved, but no specific seat is assigned.

Things to Consider: Pew cards may be inserted along with the invitation, or may be sent separately after the RSVPs have been returned. It is often easier to send them after you have received all RSVPs so you know how many reserved pews will be needed.

Tips to Save Money: Include the pew card with the invitation to special guests and just say, "Within the Ribbon." After you have received all your RSVPs, you will know how many pews need to be reserved. This will save you the cost of mailing the pew cards separately.

Price Range: $0.25 - $1 each

SEATING/PLACE CARDS

Seating/place cards are used to let guests know where they

should be seated at the reception and are a good way of putting people together so they feel most comfortable. Place cards should be laid out alphabetically on a table at the entrance to the reception. Each card should correspond to a table—either by number, color, or other identifying factor. Each table should be marked accordingly.

Options: Select a traditional or contemporary design for your place cards, depending on the style of your wedding. Regardless of the design, place cards must contain the same information: the bride and groom's names on the first line; the date on the second line; the third line is left blank for you to write in the guest's name; and the fourth line is for the table number, color, or other identifying factor.

Price Range: $0.25 - $1 each

RAIN CARDS

These cards are enclosed when guests are invited to an outdoor ceremony and/or reception, informing them of an alternate location in case of bad weather. As with other enclosures, rain cards should be placed in front of the invitation, facing the back flap and the person inserting them. They should be printed on the same quality paper and in the same style as the invitation itself.

Price Range: $0.25 - $1 each

MAPS

Maps to the ceremony and/or reception are becoming frequent inserts in wedding invitations. They need to be drawn and printed in the same style as the invitation and are usually on a small, heavier card. If they are not printed in the same style or on the same type of paper as the invitation, they should be mailed separately.

Options: Maps should include both written and visual instructions, keeping in mind the fact that guests may be coming from different locations.

Things to Consider: Order extra maps to hand out at the ceremony if the reception is at a different location.

Tips to Save Money: If you are comfortable with computers, you can purchase software that allows you to draw your own maps. Print a map to both the ceremony and reception on the same sheet of paper, perhaps one on each side. This will save you the cost of mailing two maps. Or have your ushers hand out maps to the reception after the ceremony.

Price Range: $0.50 - $1 each

CEREMONY PROGRAMS

Ceremony programs are printed documents showing the sequence of events during the ceremony. These programs add a personal touch to your wedding and are a convenient way of letting guests know who your attendants, officiant, and ceremony musicians are.

Options: Ceremony programs can be handed out by the ushers, or they can be placed at the back of the church for guests to take as they enter.

Price Range: $0.75 - $3 each

ANNOUNCEMENTS

Announcements are not obligatory but serve a useful purpose. They may be sent to friends who are not invited to the wedding because the number of guests must be limited or because they live too far away. They may also be sent to acquaintances who, while not particularly close to the family, might still wish to know about the marriage.

Announcements are also appropriate for friends and acquaintances who are not expected to attend and for whom you do not want to give an obligation of sending a gift. They should include the day, month, year, city, and state where the ceremony took place.

Things to Consider: Announcements should never be sent to anyone who has received an invitation to the ceremony or the reception. They are printed on the same paper and in the same style as the invitation. They should be addressed before the wedding and mailed the day of or the day after the ceremony.

Price Range: $0.75 - $2 each

THANK-YOU NOTES

Regardless of whether the bride has thanked the donor in person or not, she must write a thank-you note for every gift received.

Things to Consider: Order thank-you notes along with your other stationery at least four months before your wedding. You should order some with your maiden initials for thank-you notes sent before the ceremony, and the rest with your married initials for notes sent after the wedding and for future use. Send thank-you notes within two weeks of receiving a gift that arrives before the wedding, and within two months after the honeymoon for gifts received on or after your wedding day. Be sure to mention the gift you received in the body of the note and let the person know how much you like it and what you plan to do with it.

Price Range: $0.40 - $0.75 each

STAMPS

Don't forget to budget stamps for response cards as well as for invitations!

Things to Consider: Don't order stamps until you have had the post office weigh your completed invitation. It may

exceed the size and weight for one stamp. Order commemo-
rative stamps that fit the occasion.

Price Range: $0.39 - $1 per each invitation

CALLIGRAPHY

Calligraphy is a form of elegant handwriting often used to
address invitations for formal occasions. Traditional wedding
invitations should be addressed in black or blue fountain
pen.

Options: You may address the invitations yourself, hire a
professional calligrapher, or have your invitations addressed
using calligraphy by computer. Make sure you use the same
method or person to address both the inner and outer envelopes.

Tips to Save Money: You may want to consider taking a
short course to learn the art of calligraphy so that you can
address your own invitations. If you have a computer with
a laser printer, you can address the invitations yourself using
one of many beautiful calligraphy fonts.
Price Range: $0.50 - $3 each

NAPKINS/MATCHBOOKS

Napkins and matchbooks may also be ordered from your
stationer. These are placed around the reception room as

decorative items and mementos of the event.

Things to Consider: Napkins and matchbooks can be printed in your wedding colors, or simply white with gold or silver lettering. Include both of your names and the wedding date. You may consider including a phrase or thought, or a small graphic design above your names.

Price Range: $0.50 - $1.50 each

- ❑ Invitations
- ❑ Envelopes
- ❑ Response Cards/Envelopes
- ❑ Reception Cards
- ❑ Pew Cards
- ❑ Seating/Place Cards
- ❑ Rain Cards
- ❑ Maps
- ❑ Ceremony Programs
- ❑ Announcements
- ❑ Thank-You Notes
- ❑ Stamps
- ❑ Personalized Napkins/Matchbooks
- ❑ Other:
- ❑ Other:
- ❑ Other:

The Marriage of
Carol Ann Smith and William James Clark
the eleventh of March, 2008
San Diego, California

OUR CEREMONY

Prelude:
All I Ask of You, by Andrew Lloyd Webber

Processional:
Canon in D Major, by Pachelbel

Rite of Marriage

Welcome guests

Statement of intentions

Marriage vows

Exchange of rings

Blessing of bride and groom

Pronouncement of marriage

Presentation of the bride and groom

Recessional:
Trumpet Voluntary, by Jeromiah Clarke

OUR WEDDING PARTY

Maid of Honor:
Susan Smith, Sister of Bride

Best Man:
Brandt Clark, Brother of Groom

Bridesmaids:
Janet Anderson, Friend of Bride
Lisa Bennett, Friend of Bride

Ushers:
Mark Gleason, Friend of Groom
Tommy Ol-n, Friend of Groom

Officiant:
Father Henry Thomas

OUR RECEPTION

Please join us after the ceremony
in the celebration of our marriage at:
La Valencia Hotel
1132 Prospect Street
La Jolla, California

STATIONERY QUESTIONNAIRE

- What is the name and phone number of the stationery provider?
- What is the website and e-mail of the stationery provider?
- What is the address of the stationery provider?
- How many years of experience do you have?
- What lines of stationery do you carry?
- What types of printing processes do you offer?
- How soon in advance does the order have to be placed?
- What is the turnaround time?
- What is the cost of the desired invitation?
- What is the cost of the desired announcement?
- What is the cost of the desired response card?
- What is the cost of the desired reception card?
- What is the cost of the desired thank-you note?
- What is the cost of the desired party favors?
- What is the cost of the desired wedding program?
- What is the cost of addressing the envelopes in calligraphy?
- What is your payment policy?
- What is your cancellation policy?

ADDRESSING INVITATIONS

WE RECOMMEND THAT YOU start addressing your invitations at least three months before your wedding, and preferably four months if you are using calligraphy or if your guest list is above 200. You may want to ask your maid of honor or bridesmaids to help you with this time-consuming task, as this is traditionally part of their responsibilities. Organize a luncheon or late afternoon get together with hors d'oeuvres and make a party out of it! If you are working with a wedding consultant, s/he can also help you address invitations.

There are typically two envelopes that need to be addressed for wedding invitations: an inner envelope and an outer envelope. The inner envelope is placed unsealed inside the outer envelope, with the flap away from the person inserting.

The invitation and all enclosures are placed inside the inner envelope facing the back flap. The inner envelope contains the name (or names) of the person (or people) who are invited to the ceremony and/or reception. The address is not included on the inner envelope. The outer envelope contains the name (or names) and address of the person (or people) to whom the inner envelope belongs.

Use the guidelines below to help you properly address both the inner and outer envelopes.

GUIDELINES FOR ADDRESSING INVITATIONS

Husband and Wife *(with same surname)*

> **Inner Envelope**
> Mr. and Mrs. Smith
>
> **Outer Envelope**
> Mr. and Mrs. Thomas Smith
> *(use middle name, if known)*

Husband and Wife *(with different surnames)*

> **Inner Envelope**
> Ms. Banks and Mr. Smith *(wife first)*
>
> **Outer Envelope**
> Ms. Anita Banks
> Mr. Thomas Smith
> *(wife's name & title above husband's)*

Husband and Wife *(wife has professional title)*

Inner Envelope
Dr. Smith and Mr. Smith

Outer Envelope
Dr. Anita Smith
Mr. Thomas Smith
(wife's name & title above husband's)

Husband and Wife *(with children under 16)*

Inner Envelope
Mr. and Mrs. Smith
John, Mary, and Glen *(in order of age)*

Outer Envelope
Mr. and Mrs. Thomas Smith

Single Woman *(regardless of age)*

Inner Envelope
Miss/Ms. Smith

Outer Envelope
Miss/Ms. Beverly Smith

Single Woman and Guest

Inner Envelope
Miss/Ms. Smith
Mr. Jones *(or "and Guest")*

Outer Envelope
Miss/Ms. Beverly Smith

Single Man

Inner Envelope
Mr. Jones *(Master for a young boy)*

Outer Envelope
Mr. William Jones

Single Man and Guest

Inner Envelope
Mr. Jones
Miss/Ms. Smith *(or "and Guest")*

Outer Envelope
Mr. William Jones

Unmarried Couple Living Together

Inner Envelope
Mr. Knight and Ms. Orlandi
(names listed alphabetically)

Outer Envelope
Mr. Michael Knight
Ms. Paula Orlandi

Two Sisters (over 16)

Inner Envelope
The Misses Smith

Outer Envelope
The Misses Mary and Jane Smith
(in order of age)

Two Brothers (over 16)

Inner Envelope
The Messrs. Smith

Outer Envelope
The Messrs. John and Glen Smith
(in order of age)

Brothers & Sisters (over 16)

Inner Envelope
Mary, Jane, John & Glen
(name the girls first, in order of age)

Outer Envelope
The Misses Smith
The Messrs. Smith
(name the girls first)

A Brother and Sister (over 16)

Inner Envelope
Jane and John (name the girl first)

Outer Envelope
Miss Jane Smith and Mr. John Smith
(name the girl first)

Widow

Inner Envelope
Mrs. Smith

Outer Envelope
Mrs. William Smith

Divorcee

Inner Envelope
Mrs. Smith

Outer Envelope
Mrs. Jones Smith
(maiden name and former husband's surname)

RECEPTION

THE RECEPTION IS A PARTY WHERE all your guests come together to celebrate your new life as a married couple. It should reflect and complement the formality of your ceremony. The selection of a reception site will depend on its availability, price, proximity to the ceremony site, and the number of people it will accommodate.

RECEPTION SITE FEE

There are two basic types of reception sites. The first type charges a per person fee that includes the facility, food, tables, silverware, china, and so forth. Examples: hotels, restaurants, and catered yachts. The second type charges a room rental fee and you are responsible for providing the food, beverages, linens, and possibly tables and chairs. Examples: clubs, halls, parks, museums, and private homes.

RECEPTION

The advantage of the first type is that almost everything is done for you. The disadvantage, however, is that your choices of food, china, and linen are limited. Usually you are not permitted to bring in an outside caterer and must select from a predetermined menu.

Options: Private homes, gardens, hotels, clubs, restaurants, halls, parks, museums, yachts, and wineries are some of the more popular choices for receptions.

Things to Consider: When comparing the cost of different locations, consider the rental fee, food, beverages, parking, gratuity, setup charges, and the cost of rental equipment needed such as tables, chairs, canopies, and so forth. If you are planning an outdoor reception, be sure to have a backup site in case of rain.

Beware: Some hotels are known for double booking. A bride may reserve the largest or most elegant room in a hotel for her reception, only to find out later that the hotel took the liberty to book a more profitable event in the room she had reserved and moved her reception over to a smaller or less elegant room.

Also be careful of hotels that book events too close together. You don't want your guests to wait outside while your room is being set up for the reception. And you don't want to be "forced out" before you are ready to leave because the hotel needs to arrange the room for the next reception. Get your rental hours and the name of your room in writing.

Tips to Save Money: Since the cost of the reception is approximately 35% of the total cost of your wedding, you can save the most money by limiting your guest list. If you hire a wedding consultant, s/he may be able to cut your cake and save you the cake-cutting fee. Check this out with your facility or caterer. Reception sites that charge a room rental fee may waive this fee if you meet minimum requirements on food and beverages consumed. Try to negotiate this before you book the facility.

Price Range: $300 - $5,000

HORS D'OEUVRES

At receptions where a full meal is to be served, hors d'oeuvres may be offered to guests during the first hour of the reception. However, at a tea or cocktail reception, hors d'oeuvres will be the "main course."

Options: There are many options for hors d'oeuvres, depending on the formality of your reception and the type of food to be served at the meal. Popular items are foods that can easily be picked up and eaten with one hand. Hors d'oeuvres may be set out on tables "buffet style" for guests to help themselves, or they may be passed around on trays by waiters and waitresses.

Things to Consider: When selecting hors d'oeuvres for your reception, consider whether heating or refrigeration will be available and choose your food accordingly. When planning your menu, consider the time of day. You should select lighter hors d'oeuvres for a midday reception and heavier hors d'oeuvres for an evening reception.

Tips to Save Money: Tray pass hors d'oeuvres during cocktail hour and serve a lighter meal. Avoid serving hors d'oeuvres that are labor intensive or that require expensive ingredients. Compare two or three caterers; there is a wide price range between caterers for the same food. Compare the total cost of catering (main entree plus hors d'oeuvres) when selecting a caterer. Consider serving hors d'oeuvres buffet style. Your guests will eat less this way than if waiters and waitresses are constantly serving them hors d'oeuvres.

Price Range: $3 - $20 per person

MAIN MEAL/CATERER

If your reception is going to be at a hotel, restaurant or other facility that provides food, you will need to select a meal to serve your guests. Most of these facilities will have a predetermined menu from which to select your meal. If your reception is going to be in a facility that does not provide food, you will need to hire an outside caterer. The caterer will be responsible for preparing, cooking, and serving the food. The caterer will also be responsible for beverages and for cleaning up after the event. Before signing a contract, make sure you understand all the services the caterer will provide. Your contract should state the amount and type of food and beverages that will be served, the way in which they will be served, the number of servers who will be available, and the cost per food item or person.

Options: Food can be served either buffet style or as a sit-down meal. It should be chosen according to the time of day, season, and formality of the wedding. Although there are many main dishes to choose from, chicken and beef are the most popular selections for a large event. Ask your facility manager or caterer for their specialty. If you have a special type of food you would like to serve at your reception, select a facility or caterer who specializes in preparing it.

Things to Consider: When hiring a caterer, check to see if the location for your reception provides refrigeration and cooking equipment. If not, make sure your caterer is fully self-supported with portable refrigeration and heating equipment. A competent caterer will prepare much of the food in his/her own kitchen and should provide an adequate staff of cooks, servers, and bartenders. Ask for references and look at photos from previous parties so you know how the food will be presented; or better yet, visit an event they are catering.

Beware: Avoid mayonnaise, cream sauces, or custard fillings if food must go unrefrigerated for any length of time.

Tips to Save Money: Give only 85 to 95 percent of your final guest count to your caterer or facility manager, depending on how certain you are that all of your guests who have responded will come. Chances are that several, if not many, of your guests will not show up. But if they do, your caterer should have enough food for all of them. This is especially true with buffet-style receptions, in which case the facility or caterer will charge extra for each additional guest. However, if you give a complete count of your guests to your caterer and some of them don't show up, you will still have to pay for their plates. If offering a buffet meal, have the catering staff serve the food onto guests' plates rather than allowing guests to serve themselves. This will help to regulate the amount of food consumed.

Select food that is not too time-consuming to prepare, or food that does not have expensive ingredients. Also, consider a brunch or early afternoon wedding so the reception will fall between meals, allowing you to serve hors d'oeuvres instead of a full meal. Or tray pass hors d'oeuvres during cocktail hour and choose a lighter meal.

Price Range: $20 - $100 per person

LIQUOR/BEVERAGES

Prices for liquor and beverages vary greatly, depending on the amount and brand of alcohol served. Traditionally, at least champagne or punch should be served to toast the couple.

Options: White and red wines, scotch, vodka, gin, rum, and beer are the most popular alcoholic beverages. Sodas and fruit punch are popular nonalcoholic beverages served at receptions. And of course, don't forget coffee or tea. There are a number of options and variations for serving alcoholic beverages: a full open bar where you pay for your guests to drink as much as they wish; an open bar for the first hour, followed by a cash bar where guests pay for their own drinks; cash bar only; beer and wine only; nonalcoholic beverages only; or any combination thereof.

Things to Consider: If you plan to serve alcoholic beverages at a reception site that does not provide liquor, make sure your caterer has a license to serve alcohol and that your reception site allows alcoholic beverages. If you plan to order your own alcohol, do so three or four weeks before the event. If you plan to have a no-host or "cash" bar, consider notifying your guests so they know to bring cash with them. A simple line that says "No-Host Bar" on the reception card should suffice.

In selecting the type of alcohol to serve, consider the age and preference of your guests, the type of food that will be served, and the time of day your guests will be drinking.

On the average, you should allow one drink per person, per hour at the reception. A bottle of champagne will usually serve six glasses. Never serve liquor without some type of food. Use the following chart to plan your beverage needs:

Beverages	Amount based on 100 guests
Bourbon	3 Fifths
Gin	3 Fifths
Rum	2 Fifths
Scotch	4 Quarts
Vodka	5 Quarts

White Wine	2 Cases
Red Wine	1 Case
Champagne	3 Cases
Other	2 Cases each:
	Club Soda, Seltzer Water,
	Tonic Water, Ginger Ale,
	Cola, Beer

If you are hosting an open bar at a hotel or restaurant, ask the catering manager how they charge for liquor: by consumption or by number of bottles opened. Get this in writing before the event and then ask for a full consumption report after the event.

Beware: In today's society, it is not uncommon for the hosts of a party to be held legally responsible for the conduct and safety of their guests. Keep this in mind when planning the quantity and type of beverages to serve. Also, be sure to remind your bartenders not to serve alcohol to minors.

Tips to Save Money: To keep beverage costs down, serve punch, wine, or nonalcoholic drinks only. If your caterer allows it, consider buying liquor from a wholesaler who will let you return unopened bottles. Also, avoid salty foods such as potato chips, pretzels, or ham. These foods will make your guests thirstier so they will tend to drink more.

Host alcoholic beverages for the first hour, then go to a cash bar. Or host beer, wine, and soft drinks only and have mixed drinks available on a cash basis. The bartending fee is often waived if you meet the minimum requirements on beverages consumed. For the toast, tray pass champagne only to those guests who want it, not to everyone. Many people will make a toast with whatever they are currently drinking. Consider serving sparkling cider in place of champagne.

Omit waiters and waitresses. Instead, have an open bar in which your guests have to get their own drinks. People tend to drink almost twice as much if there are waiters and waitresses constantly asking them if they would like another drink and then bringing drinks to them.

Price Range: $8 - $35 per person

BARTENDING/BAR SETUP FEE

Some reception sites and caterers charge an extra fee for bartending and for setting up the bar.

Tips to Save Money: The bartending fee could be and often is waived if you meet a minimum requirement on beverages consumed. Try to negotiate this with your caterer prior to hiring him/her.

Price Range: $75 - $500

CORKAGE FEE

Many reception sites and caterers make money by marking up the food and alcohol they sell. You may wish to provide your own alcohol for several reasons. First, it is more cost effective. Second, you may want to serve an exotic wine or champagne that the reception site or caterer does not offer. In either case, and if your reception site or caterer allows it, be prepared to pay a corkage fee. This is the fee for each bottle brought into the reception site and opened by a member of their staff.

Things to Consider: You need to consider whether the expenses saved after paying the corkage fee justify the hassle and liability of bringing in your own alcohol.

Price Range: $5 - $20 per bottle

FEE TO POUR COFFEE

In addition to corkage and cake-cutting fees, some facilities also charge extra to pour coffee with the wedding cake.

Things to Consider: Again, when comparing the cost of various reception sites, don't forget to add up all the extra miscellaneous costs, such as the fee for pouring coffee.

Price Range: $0.25 - $1 per person

SERVICE PROVIDERS' MEALS

Things to Consider: It is considered a courtesy to feed your photographer, videographer, and any other "service provider" at the reception. Check options and prices with your caterer or reception site manager. Make sure you allocate a place for your service providers to eat. You may want them to eat with your guests, or you may prefer setting a place outside the main room for them to eat. Your service providers may be more comfortable with the latter.

Tips to Save Money: You don't need to feed your service providers the same meal as your guests. You can order sandwiches or another less expensive meal for them. If the meal is a buffet, there should be enough food left after all your guests have been served for your service providers to eat. Tell them they are welcome to eat after all your guests have been served. Be sure to discuss this with your catering manager.

Price Range: $10 - $30 per person

GRATUITY

It is customary to pay a gratuity fee to your caterer. The average gratuity is 15 percent to 20 percent of your food and beverage bill.

Tips to Save Money: Ask about these costs up front and select your caterer or reception site accordingly.

Price Range: 15 - 25 percent of total food and beverage bill

PARTY FAVORS

Party favors are little gift items given to your guests as mementos of your wedding. They add a very special touch to your wedding and can become keepsakes for your guests.

Options: White matchboxes engraved with the couple's names and wedding date; cocktail napkins marked in the same way; individually wrapped and marked chocolates, almonds, or fine candy are all popular party favors. Wine or champagne bottles marked with the bride and groom's names and wedding date on a personalized label are also very popular. These come in different sizes and can be purchased by the case.

If you can afford it, you may also consider porcelain or ceramic party favors. These can be custom-fired with your name and wedding date on them. A new idea that's gaining in popularity among environmentally conscientious couples is to present each guest with a tiny shoot of an endangered tree to be planted in honor of the bride and groom.

Things to Consider: Personalized favors need to be ordered several weeks in advance.

Price Range: $1 - $25 per person

DISPOSABLE CAMERAS

A great way to inexpensively obtain many candid photographs of your wedding day is to place a disposable 35mm camera loaded with film on each table at your reception, and to have your guests take shots of the event! Disposable cameras come preloaded with film. Your guests can leave the cameras at their table or drop them in a basket or other labeled container near the entrance to the reception site. Arrange for someone to collect the cameras after the event. Tell your DJ, musician, or wedding coordinator to encourage your guests to take photographs with the disposables. You will end up with many beautiful, memorable and candid photographs of your reception.

Things to Consider: Disposable cameras are sold with and without flash. Disposable cameras with flash are more expensive but necessary if your reception is going to be held indoors or in the evening. If you are planning a large reception, consider buying cameras with only twelve exposures. Otherwise, you may end up with too many photographs. For example, if 200 guests attend your reception and you seat eight guests per table, you will need to purchase 25 cameras. If each camera has 36 exposures, you will end up with 825 photographs. If the cameras have only twelve exposures, you will end up with 300 photographs, which is a much more reasonable quantity!

Tips to Save Money: Instead of developing these photographs into print and then placing them into a big album, have your videographer transfer the negatives directly onto video set to your favorite music. You can then reproduce this "photo montage" and send it as a gift to your friends and family members. You can later decide which of these photographs you want to develop into print.

Price Range: $4 - $20 per camera

ROSE PETALS/RICE

Rose petals or rice are traditionally tossed over the bride and groom as they leave the church after the ceremony or when they leave the reception. These are usually handed out to guests in little sachet bags while the bride and groom are changing into their going away clothes. This tradition was initiated in the Middle Ages whereby a handful of wheat was thrown over the bridal couple as a symbol of fertility. Rose petals are used to symbolize happiness, beauty, and prosperity.

Options: Rose petals, rice, or confetti are often used. However, an environmentally correct alternative is to use grass or flower seeds, which do not need to be "cleaned up" if tossed over a grassy area. These come wrapped in attractive, recycled packages with the couple's names and wedding date printed on the front.

Things to Consider: Rose petals can stain carpets; rice can sting faces, harm birds and make stairs dangerously slippery; confetti is messy and hard to clean. Clubs and hotels seldom permit the use of any of these. Ask about their policy.

Price Range: $0.35 - $2 per person

GIFT ATTENDANT

The gift attendant is responsible for watching over your gifts during the reception so that no one walks away with them. This is necessary only if your reception is held in a public area such as a hotel or outside garden where strangers may be walking by. It is not proper to have a friend or family member take on this duty as s/he would not enjoy the reception. The gift attendant should also be responsible for transporting your gifts from the reception site to your car or bridal suite.

Tips to Save Money: Hire a young boy or girl from your neighborhood to watch over your gifts at the reception.

Price Range: $20 - $100

PARKING FEE/VALET SERVICES

Many reception sites such as hotels, restaurants, etc., charge for parking. It is customary, although not necessary, for the host of the wedding to pay this charge. At a large home reception, you should consider hiring a professional, qualified valet service if parking could be a problem. If so, make sure the valet service is fully insured.

Things to Consider: When comparing the cost of reception sites, don't forget to add the cost of parking to the total price.

Tips to Save Money: To save money, let your guests pay their own parking fees.

Price Range: $3 - $10 per car

- What is the name of the reception site?
- What is the website and e-mail of the reception site?
- What is the address of the reception site?
- What is the name and phone number of my contact person?
- What dates and times are available?
- What is the maximum number of guests for a seated reception?
- What is the maximum number of guests for a cocktail reception?
- What is the reception site fee?
- What is the price range for a seated lunch?
- What is the price range for a buffet lunch?
- What is the price range for a seated dinner?
- What is the price range for a buffet dinner?
- What is the corkage fee?
- What is the cake-cutting fee?
- What is the ratio of servers to guests?
- How much time will be allotted for my reception?
- What music restrictions are there, if any?
- What alcohol restrictions are there, if any?
- Are there any restrictions for rice or rose petal tossing?
- What room and table decorations are available?
- Is a changing room available?
- Is there handicap accessibility?
- Is a dance floor included in the site fee?
- Are tables, chairs, and linens included in the site fee?
- Are outside caterers allowed?
- Are kitchen facilities available for outside caterers?

RECEPTION SITE QUESTIONNAIRE CONT.

- Does the facility have full liability insurance?
- What perks or giveaways are offered?
- How many parking spaces are available for my wedding party?
- How many parking spaces are available for my guests?
- What is the cost for parking, if any?
- What is the cost for sleeping rooms, if available?
- What is the payment policy?
- What is the cancellation policy?

- What is the name of the caterer?
- What is the website and e-mail of the caterer?
- What is the address of the caterer?
- What is the name and phone number of my contact person?
- How many years have you been in business?
- What percentage of your business is dedicated to receptions?
- Do you have liability insurance/license to serve alcohol?
- When is the final head-count needed?
- What is your ratio of servers to guests?
- How do your servers dress for wedding receptions?
- What is your price range for a seated lunch/buffet lunch?
- What is your price range for a seated/buffet dinner?
- How much gratuity is expected?
- What is your specialty?
- What is your cake-cutting fee?
- What is your bartending fee?
- What is your fee to clean up after the reception?
- What is your payment policy?
- What is your cancellation policy?

MUSIC

CEREMONY MUSIC IS THE MUSIC played during the prelude, processional, ceremony, recessional, and postlude. Prelude music is played while guests are being seated, 15 to 30 minutes before the ceremony begins. Processional music is played as the wedding party enters the ceremony site. Recessional music is played as the wedding party leaves the ceremony site. Postlude music is played while the guests leave the ceremony site.

CEREMONY MUSIC

Options: The most traditional musical instrument for wedding ceremonies is the organ. But guitars, pianos, flutes, harps, and violins are also popular today.

Popular selections for a Christian wedding:

Trumpet Voluntary by Purcell
The Bridal Chorus by Wagner
Wedding March by Mendelssohn

Postlude in G Major by Handel
Canon in D Major by Pachelbel
Adagio in A Minor by Bach

Popular selections for a Jewish wedding:

Erev Shel Shoshanim
Erev Ba
Hana' Ava Babanot

Things to Consider: Music may or may not be included as part of the ceremony site fee. Be sure to check with your ceremony site about restrictions pertaining to music and the availability of musical instruments for your use. Discuss the selection of ceremony music with your officiant and musicians. Make sure the musicians know how to play the selections you request.

When selecting ceremony music, keep in mind the formality of your wedding, your religious affiliation, and the length of the ceremony. Also consider the location and time of day. If the ceremony is outside where there may be other noises such as traffic, wind, or people's voices, or if a large number of guests will be attending your ceremony, consider having the music, your officiant, and your vows amplified. Make sure there are electrical outlets close to where the instruments will be set up.

Tips to Save Money: Hire student musicians from your local university or high school. Ask a friend to sing or play at your ceremony; they will be honored. If you're planning to hire a band for your reception, consider hiring a scaled-down version of the same band to play at your ceremony, such as a trio of flute, guitar, and vocals. This could enable you to negotiate a "package" price. If you're planning to hire a DJ for your reception, consider hiring him/her to play pre-recorded music at your ceremony.

Price Range: $100 - $900

RECEPTION MUSIC

Music is a major part of your reception, and should be planned carefully. Music helps create the atmosphere of your wedding. Special songs will make your reception unique. When you select music for your reception, keep in mind the age and musical preference of your guests, your budget, and any restrictions that the reception site may have. Bands and musicians are typically more expensive than DJs.

Options: There are many options for reception music: you can hire a DJ, a band, an orchestra, or any combination of one or more instruments and vocalists.

Things to Consider: Hire an entertainment agency that can help you choose a reliable DJ or band that will play the type of music you want. Whoever you choose, they should have experience performing at wedding receptions.

If you want your musician to act as a master of ceremonies, make sure s/he has a complete timeline for your reception in order to announce the various events such as the toasts, first dance, and cutting of the cake. Consider watching your musicians perform at another event before booking their services.

If you need a large variety of music to satisfy all your guests, consider hiring a DJ. A professional DJ can play any type of music and may even offer a light show. Make sure you give him/her a list of the songs you want played at your reception and the sequence in which you want them played. Make sure there are electrical outlets at the reception site close to where the musicians will be performing.

Tips to Save Money: You will probably get a better price if you hire a band or DJ directly than if you hire them through an entertainment agency. Check the music department of local colleges and universities for names of student musicians and DJs. You may be able to hire a student for a fraction of the price of a professional musician or DJ. A DJ is typically less expensive than a "live" musician. Some facilities have contracts with certain DJs, and you may be able to save money by hiring one of them.

Price Range: $500 - $5,000

Bonus Tip: For suggestions on appropriate music for each moment of the wedding, you should consider purchasing The Ultimate Guide to Wedding Music from Wedding Solutions. This book contains lyrics for 100 of the most popular love songs for weddings. It also includes an audio CD with excerpts from 99 of the most popular classical music pieces for weddings.

CEREMONY MUSIC QUESTIONNAIRE

- What is the name of the musician or band?
- What is the website and e-mail of the musician or band?
- What is the address of the musician or band?
- What is the name and phone number of my contact person?
- How many years of professional experience do you have?
- What percentage of your business is dedicated to weddings?
- Are you the person who will perform at my wedding?
- What instrument(s) do you play?
- What type of music do you specialize in?
- What are your hourly fees?
- What is the cost of a soloist?
- What is the cost of a duet?
- What is the cost of a trio?
- What is the cost of a quartet?
- How would you dress for my wedding?
- Do you have liability insurance?
- Do you have a cordless microphone?
- What is your payment/cancellation policy?

RECEPTION MUSIC QUESTIONNAIRE

- What is the name of the musician? Band? DJ?
- What is the website and e-mail of the musician? Band? DJ?
- What is the address of the musician? Band? DJ?
- What is the name and phone number of my contact person?
- How many years of professional experience do you have?
- What percentage of your business is dedicated to receptions?
- How many people are in your band?
- What type of music do you specialize in?
- What type of sound system do you have?
- Can you act as a master of ceremonies? How do you dress?
- Can you provide a light show?
- Do you have a cordless microphone?
- How many breaks do you take? How long are they?
- Do you play recorded music during breaks?
- Do you have liability insurance?
- What are your fees for a 4-hour reception?
- What is your cost for each additional hour?

BAKERY

WEDDING CAKES MAY BE ordered from a caterer or from a bakery. Some hotels and restaurants may also be able to provide a wedding cake. However, you will probably be better off ordering your cake from a bakery that specializes in wedding cakes. Ask to see photographs of other wedding cakes your baker has created, and by all means, ask for a tasting!

WEDDING CAKE

Options: When ordering your cake, you will have to decide not only on a flavor, but also on a size, shape, and color. Size is determined by the number of guests. You can choose from one large tier or more smaller tiers. The cake can be round, square, or heart-shaped. The most common flavors are chocolate, carrot, lemon, rum, and "white" cakes. You can be creative by adding a filling to your cake, such as custard, strawberry, or chocolate. You may also want to consider having tiers of different flavors.

Things to Consider: Price, workmanship, quality, and taste vary considerably from baker to baker. In addition to flavor, size, and cost, consider decoration and spoilage (sugar keeps longer than cream frostings). The cake should be beautifully displayed on its own table decorated with flowers or greenery. Make sure the baker, caterer, or reception site manager can provide you with a pretty cake-cutting knife. If not, you will need to purchase or rent one.

When determining the size of the cake, don't forget that you'll be saving the top tier for your first anniversary. This top tier should be removed before the cake is cut, wrapped in several layers of plastic wrap or put inside a plastic container, and kept frozen until your anniversary.

Tips to Save Money: Some bakers have setup and delivery fees, and some don't. Check for individuals who bake from their home. They are usually more reasonable, but you should check with your local health department before hiring one of these at-home bakers. Also, some caterers have contracts with bakeries and can pass on savings to you. Some bakeries require a deposit on columns and plates; other bakeries use disposable columns and plates, saving you the rental fee and the hassle of returning these items.

Price Range: $2 - $12 per piece

GROOM'S CAKE

The groom's cake is an old southern tradition whereby this cake is cut up and distributed to guests in little white boxes engraved with the bride and groom's names. Today the groom's cake, if offered, is cut and served along with the wedding cake.

Options: Usually a chocolate cake decorated with fruit.

Tips to Save Money: Because of its cost and the labor involved in cutting and distributing the cake, very few people offer this delightful custom any more.

Price Range: $1 - $2 per piece

CAKE DELIVERY/SETUP FEE

This is the fee charged by bakers to deliver and set up your wedding cake at the reception site. It usually includes a deposit on the cake pillars and plate which will be refunded upon their return to the baker.

Tips to Save Money: Have a friend or family member get a quick lesson on how to set up your cake. Have them pick it up and set it up the day of your wedding, then have the florist decorate the cake and/or cake table with flowers and greenery.

Price Range: $40 - $100

CAKE-CUTTING FEE

Most reception sites and caterers charge a fee for each slice of cake they cut if the cake is brought in from an outside bakery. This fee will probably shock you. It is simply their way of enticing you to order the cake through them. Unfortunately, many caterers will not allow a member of your party to cut the cake.

Tips to Save Money: Many hotels and restaurants include a dessert in the cost of their meal packages. If you forego this dessert and substitute your cake as the dessert, they may be willing to waive the cake-cutting fee. Be sure to ask them.

Price Range: $0.75 - $2.50 per person

CAKE TOP

The bride's cake is often topped and surrounded with fresh flowers, but traditional "cake tops" (figurines set atop the wedding cake) are also very popular.

Options: Bells, love birds, a bridal couple or replica of two wedding rings are popular choices for cake tops and can be saved as mementos of your wedding day.

Beware: Some porcelain and other heavier cake tops need to be anchored down into the cake. If you're planning to use a cake top other than flowers, be sure to discuss this with your baker.

Tips to Save Money: Borrow a cake top from a friend or a family member as "something borrowed," an age-old wedding tradition (see page 250).

Price Range: $20 - $150

CAKE KNIFE/TOASTING GLASSES

Your cake knife and toasting glasses should complement your overall setting; these items will bring you happy memories of your wedding day every time you use them. The cake knife is used to cut the cake at the reception. The bride usually cuts the first two slices of the wedding cake with the groom's hand placed over hers. The groom feeds the bride first. Then the bride feeds the groom. This tradition makes beautiful wedding photographs.

You will need toasting glasses to toast each other after cutting the cake. They are usually decorated with ribbons or flowers and kept near the cake. This tradition also makes beautiful wedding photographs.

Things to Consider: Consider having your initials and wedding date engraved on your wedding knife as a memento. Consider purchasing crystal or silver toasting glasses as a keepsake of your wedding. Have your florist decorate your knife and toasting glasses with flowers or ribbons.

Tips to Save Money: Borrow your cake knife or toasting glasses from a friend or family member as "something borrowed," an age-old wedding tradition (see page 250). Use the reception facility's glasses and knife, and decorate them with flowers or ribbon.

**Price Range: $15 - $120 for knife;
$10 - $100 for toasting glasses**

- What is the name of the bakery?
- What is the bakery's website and e-mail?
- What is the address of the bakery?
- What is the name and phone number of my contact person?
- How many years have you been making wedding cakes?
- What are your wedding cake specialties?
- Do you offer free tasting of your wedding cakes?
- Are your wedding cakes fresh or frozen?
- How far in advance should I order my cake?
- Can you make a groom's cake?
- Do you lend, rent, or sell cake knives?
- What is the cost per serving of my desired cake?
- What is your cake pillar and plate rental fee, if any?
- Is this fee refundable upon the return of these items?
- When must these items be returned?
- What is your cake delivery and setup fee?
- What is your payment policy?
- What is your cancellation policy?

FLOWERS

Flowers add beauty, fragrance, and color to your wedding. Like everything else, flowers should fit your overall style and color scheme. The purpose of flowers at the main altar is to direct the guests' visual attention toward the front of the church and to the bridal couple. Therefore, they must be seen by guests seated toward the back. You may also want to use flowers or ribbons to mark the aisle pews and add color.

BRIDE'S BOUQUET

The bridal bouquet is one of the most important elements of the bride's attire and deserves special attention. Start by selecting the color and shape of the bouquet. The bridal bouquet should be carried low enough so that all the intricate details of your gown are visible.

FLOWERS

Options: There are many colors, scents, sizes, shapes, and styles of bouquets to choose from. Popular styles are the cascade, cluster, contemporary, and hand-tied garden bouquets. The traditional bridal bouquet is made of white flowers. Stephanotis, gardenias, white roses, orchids, and lilies of the valley are popular choices for an all-white bouquet.

If you prefer a colorful bouquet, you may want to consider using roses, tulips, stock, peonies, freesia, and gerbera, which come in a wide variety of colors. Using scented flowers in your bouquet will evoke memories of your wedding day whenever you smell them in the future. Popular fragrant flowers are gardenias, freesia, stephanotis, bouvardia, and narcissus. Select flowers that are in season to assure availability (see pages 173-211).

Things to Consider: Your flowers should complement the season, your gown, your color scheme, your attendants' attire, and the style and formality of your wedding. If you have a favorite flower, build your bouquet around it and include it in all your arrangements. Some flowers carry centuries of symbolism. Consider stephanotis—tradition regards it as the bridal good-luck flower! Pimpernel signifies change; white flowers radiate innocence; forget-me-nots indicate true love; and ivy stands for friendship, fidelity, and matrimony—the three essentials for a happy marriage.

No flower, however, has as much symbolism for brides as the orange blossom, having at least 700 years of nuptial history. Its unusual ability to simultaneously bear flowers and produce fruit symbolizes the fusion of beauty, personality, and fertility.

Whatever flowers you select, final arrangements should be made well in advance of your wedding date to insure availability. Confirm your final order and delivery time a few days before the wedding. Have the flowers delivered before the photographer arrives so that you can include them in your pre-ceremony photos.

In determining the size of your bouquet, consider your gown and your overall stature. Carry a smaller bouquet if you're petite or if your gown is fairly ornate. A long, cascading bouquet complements a fairly simple gown or a tall or larger bride. Arm bouquets look best when resting naturally in the crook of your arm.

For a natural, fresh-picked look, have your florist put together a cluster of flowers tied together with a ribbon. For a Victorian appeal, carry a nosegay or a basket filled with flowers. Or carry a Bible or other family heirloom decorated with just a few flowers. For a contemporary look, you may want to consider carrying an arrangement of calla lilies or other long-stemmed flower over your arm. For a dramatic statement, carry a single stem of your favorite flower!

Beware: If your bouquet includes delicate flowers that will not withstand hours of heat or a lack of water, make sure your florist uses a bouquet holder to keep them fresh. If you want to carry fresh-cut stems without a bouquet holder, make sure the flowers you select are hardy enough to go without water for the duration of your ceremony and reception.

Tips to Save Money: The cost of some flowers may be

significantly higher during their off season. Try to select flowers that are in bloom and plentiful at the time of your wedding. Avoid exotic, out-of-season flowers. Allow your florist to emphasize your colors using more reasonable, seasonal flowers to achieve your overall look. If you have a favorite flower that is costly or out of season, consider using silk for that one flower.

Avoid scheduling your wedding on holidays such as Valentine's Day and Mother's Day when the price of flowers is higher. Because every attendant will carry or wear flowers, consider keeping the size of your wedding party down to accommodate your floral budget.

Price Range: $75 - $400

TOSSING BOUQUET

If you want to preserve your bridal bouquet, consider having your florist make a smaller, less expensive bouquet specifically for tossing. This will be the bouquet you toss to your single, female friends toward the end of the reception. Tradition has it that the woman who catches the bouquet is the next to be married. Have your florist include a few sprigs of fresh ivy in the tossing bouquet to symbolize friendship and fidelity.

Tips to Save Money: Use the floral cake top or guest book table "tickler bouquet" as the tossing bouquet. Or omit the tossing bouquet altogether and simply toss your bridal bouquet.

Price Range: $20 - $100

MAID OF HONOR'S BOUQUET

The maid of honor's bouquet can be somewhat larger or of a different color than the rest of the bridesmaids' bouquets. This will help to set her apart from the others.

Price Range: $25 - $100

BRIDESMAIDS' BOUQUETS

The bridesmaids' bouquets should complement the bridal bouquet, but are generally smaller in size. The size and color should coordinate with the bridesmaids' dresses and the overall style of the wedding. Bridesmaids' bouquets are usually identical.

Options: To personalize your bridesmaids' bouquets, insert a different flower in each of their bouquets to make a statement. For example, if one of your bridesmaids has been sad, give her a lily of the valley to symbolize the return of happiness. To tell a friend that you admire her, insert yellow jasmine. A pansy will let your friend know that you are thinking of her.

Things to Consider: Choose a bouquet style (cascade, cluster, contemporary, hand-tied) that complements the formality of your wedding and the height of your attendants. If your bridesmaids will be wearing floral print dresses, select flowers that complement the floral print.

Tips to Save Money: Have your attendants carry a single stemmed rose, lily, or other suitable flower for an elegant look that also saves money.

Price Range: $25 - $100

MAID OF HONOR/BRIDESMAIDS' HAIRPIECE

For a garden look, have your maid of honor and bridesmaids wear garlands of flowers in their hair. If so, provide your maid of honor with a slightly different color or variety of flower to set her apart from the others.

Options: You may consider using artificial flowers for the hairpieces as long as they are in keeping with the flowers carried by members of the bridal party. Since it is not always easy to find good artificial blooms, other types of hairpieces may be more satisfactory, durable, and attractive.

Things to Consider: Flowers used for the hairpiece must be a sturdy and long-lived variety.

Price Range: $8 - $100

FLOWER GIRL'S HAIRPIECE

Flower girls often wear a wreath of flowers as a hairpiece.

Options: This is another place where artificial flowers may be used, but they must be in keeping with the flowers carried by members of the bridal party. Since it is not always easy to find good artificial blooms, other types of hairpieces may be more satisfactory, durable, and attractive.

Things to Consider: If the flowers used for the hairpiece are not a sturdy and long-lived variety, a ribbon, bow, or hat might be a safer choice.

Price Range: $8 - $75

BRIDE'S GOING AWAY CORSAGE

You may want to consider wearing a corsage on your going away outfit. This makes for pretty photos as you and your new husband leave the reception for your honeymoon. Have your florist create a corsage which echoes the beauty of your bouquet.

Beware: Put a protective shield under lilies when using them as a corsage, as their anthers will easily stain fabric. Be careful when using alstroemeria as a corsage, as its sap can be harmful if it enters the human bloodstream.

Tips to Save Money: Ask your florist if s/he can design your bridal bouquet in such a way that the center flowers may be removed and worn as a corsage. Or omit this corsage altogether.

Price Range: $10 - $50

FAMILY MEMBERS' CORSAGES

The groom is responsible for providing flowers for his mother, the bride's mother, and the grandmothers. The officiant, if female, may also be given a corsage to reflect her important role in the ceremony. The corsages don't have to be identical, but they should be coordinated with the color of their dresses.

Options: The groom may order flowers that can be pinned to a pocketbook or worn around a wrist. He should ask which style the women prefer, and if a particular color is needed to coordinate with their dresses. Gardenias, camellias, white orchids, or cymbidium orchids are excellent choices for corsages, as they go well with any outfit.

Things to Consider: The groom may also want to consider ordering corsages for other close family members, such as sisters and aunts. This will add a little to your floral expenses but will make these female family members feel more included in your wedding and will let guests know that they are related to the bride and groom. Many women do not like to wear corsages, so the groom should check with the people involved before ordering the flowers.

Beware: Put a protective shield under lilies when using them as corsages, as their anthers will easily stain fabric. Be careful when using alstroemeria as corsages, as its sap can be harmful if it enters the human bloodstream.

Tips to Save Money: Ask your florist to recommend reasonable flowers for corsages. Dendrobium orchids are reasonable and make lovely corsages.

Price Range: $10 - $35

GROOM'S BOUTONNIERE

The groom wears his boutonniere on the left lapel, nearest to his heart.

Options: Boutonnieres are generally a single blossom such as a rosebud, stephanotis, freesia, or a miniature carnation. If a rosebud is used for the wedding party, have the groom wear two rosebuds, or add a sprig of baby's breath to differentiate him from the groomsmen.

Things to Consider: You may use a small cluster of flowers instead of a single bloom for the groom's boutonniere.

Beware: Be careful when using alstroemeria as a boutonniere, as its sap can be harmful if it enters the human bloodstream.

Tips to Save Money: Use mini-carnations rather than roses.

FLOWERS

Price Range: $4 - $25

USHERS/OTHER FAMILY MEMBERS' BOUTONNIERES

The groom gives each man in his wedding party a boutonniere to wear on his left lapel. The officiant, if male, may also be given a boutonniere to reflect his important role in the ceremony. The ring bearer may or may not wear a boutonniere, depending on his outfit. A boutonniere is more appropriate on a tuxedo than on knickers and knee socks.

Options: Generally, a single blossom such as a rosebud, freesia, or miniature carnation is used as a boutonniere.

Things to Consider: The groom should also consider ordering boutonnieres for other close family members such as fathers, grandfathers, and brothers. This will add a little to your floral expenses, but will make these male family members feel more included in your wedding and will let guests know that they are related to the bride and groom.

Beware: Be careful when using alstroemeria as boutonnieres, as its sap can be harmful if it enters the human bloodstream.

Tips to Save Money: Use mini-carnations rather than roses.

Price Range: $3 - $15

MAIN ALTAR

The purpose of flowers at the main altar is to direct the guests' visual attention toward the front of the church or synagogue and to the bridal couple. Therefore, they must be seen by guests seated in the back. The flowers for the ceremony site can be as elaborate or as simple as you wish. Your officiant's advice, or that of the altar guild or florist, can be most helpful in choosing flowers for the altar and chancel.

Options: If your ceremony is outside, decorate the arch, gazebo, or other structure serving as the altar with flowers or greenery. In a Jewish ceremony, vows are said under a Chuppah, which is placed at the altar and covered with greens and fresh flowers.

Things to Consider: In choosing floral accents, consider the decor of your ceremony site. Some churches and synagogues are ornate enough and don't need extra flowers. Too many arrangements would get lost in the architectural splendor. Select a few dramatic showpieces that will complement the existing decor. Be sure to ask if there are any restrictions on flowers at the church or synagogue. Remember, decorations should be determined by the size and style of the building, the formality of the wedding, the preferences of the bride, the cost, and the regulations of the particular site.

Tips to Save Money: Decorate the ceremony site with greenery only. Candlelight and greenery are elegant in and of themselves. Use greenery and flowers from your garden. Have your ceremony outside in a beautiful garden or by the water, surrounded by nature's own splendor.

Price Range: $50 - $3,000

ALTAR CANDELABRA

In a candlelight ceremony, the candelabra may be decorated with flowers or greens for a dramatic effect.

Options: Ivy may be twined around the candelabra, or flowers may be strung to them.

Price Range: $50 - $200

AISLE PEWS

Flowers, candles, or ribbons are often used to mark the aisle pews and add color.

Options: A cluster of flowers, a cascade of greens, or a cascade of flowers and ribbons are all popular choices. Candles with adorning greenery add an elegant touch.

Things to Consider: Use hardy flowers that can tolerate being handled as pew ornaments. Gardenias and camellias, for example, are too sensitive to last long.

Beware: Avoid using allium in your aisle pew decorations as they have an odor of onions.

Tips to Save Money: It is not necessary to decorate all of the aisle pews, or any at all. To save money, decorate only the reserved family pews. Or decorate every second or third pew.

Price Range: $5 - $75

RECEPTION SITE

Flowers add beauty, fragrance, and color to your reception. Flowers for the reception, like everything else, should fit your overall style and color scheme. Flowers can help transform a stark reception hall into a warm, inviting, and colorful room.

Things to Consider: You can rent indoor plants or small trees to give your reception a garden-like atmosphere. Decorate them with twinkle lights to achieve a magical effect.

Tips to Save Money: You can save money by taking flowers from the ceremony to the reception site for decorations. However, you must coordinate this move carefully to avoid having your guests arrive at an undecorated reception room. Use greenery rather than flowers to fill large areas. Trees and garlands of ivy can give a dramatic impact for little money. Use greenery and flowers from your garden. Have your reception outside in a beautiful garden or by the water, surrounded by nature's own beauty.

Price Range: $300 - $3,000

FLOWERS

HEAD TABLE

The head table is where the wedding party will sit during the reception. This important table should be decorated with a larger or more dramatic centerpiece than the guest tables.

Things to Consider: Consider using a different color or style of arrangement to set the head table apart from the other tables.

Beware: Avoid using highly fragrant flowers, such as narcissus, on tables where food is being served or eaten, as their fragrance may conflict with other aromas.

Tips to Save Money: Decorate the head table with the bridal and attendants' bouquets.

Price Range: $100 - $600

GUEST TABLES

At a reception where guests are seated, a small flower arrangement may be placed on each table.

Things to Consider: The arrangements should complement the table linens and the size of the table, and should be kept low enough so as not to hinder conversation among guests seated across from each other.

Beware: Avoid using highly fragrant flowers, like narcissus, on tables where food is being served or eaten, as their fragrance may conflict with other aromas.

Tips to Save Money: To keep the cost down and for less formal receptions, use small potted flowering plants placed in white baskets, or consider using dried or silk arrangements that you can make yourself and give later as gifts. Or place a wreath of greenery entwined with colored ribbon in the center of each table. Use a different colored ribbon at each table and assign your guests to tables by ribbon color instead of number.

Price Range: $10 - $100

BUFFET TABLE

If buffet tables are used, have some type of floral arrangement on the tables to add color and beauty to your display of food.

Options: Whole fruits and bunches of berries offer a variety of design possibilities. Figs add a festive touch. Pineapples are a sign of hospitality. Vegetables offer an endless array of options to decorate with. Herbs are yet another option in decorating. A mixture of rosemary and mint combined with scented geraniums makes a very unique table decoration.

Things to Consider: Depending on the size of the table, place one or two arrangements at each side.

Beware: Avoid placing certain flowers, such as carnations, snapdragons, or the star of Bethlehem, next to buffet displays of fruits or vegetables, as they are extremely sensitive to the gasses emitted by these foods.

Price Range: $50 - $500

PUNCH TABLE

Put an assortment of greens or a small arrangement of flowers at the punch table. See "Buffet Table."

Price Range: $10 - $100

CAKE TABLE

The wedding cake is often the central location at the reception. Decorate the cake table with flowers.

Tips to Save Money: Have your bridesmaids place their bouquets on the cake table during the reception, or decorate the cake top only and surround the base with greenery and a few loose flowers.

Price Range: $30 - $300

CAKE

Flowers are a beautiful addition to a wedding cake and are commonly seen spilling out between the cake tiers.

Things to Consider: Use only nonpoisonous flowers, and have your florist—not the caterer—design the floral decorations for your cake. A florist will be able to blend the cake decorations into your overall floral theme.

Price Range: $20 - $100

CAKE KNIFE

Decorate your cake knife with a white satin ribbon and flowers.

Things to Consider: Consider engraving the cake knife with your names and wedding date.

Price Range: $5 - $35

TOASTING GLASSES

Tie small flowers with white ribbon onto the stems of your champagne glasses. These wedding accessories deserve a special floral touch since they will most likely be included in your special photographs.

Things to Consider: Consider engraving your toasting glasses with your names and wedding date.

Price Range: $10 - $35

FLORAL DELIVERY/SETUP

Most florists charge a fee to deliver flowers to the ceremony and reception sites and to arrange them on site.

Things to Consider: Make sure your florist knows where your sites are and what time to arrive for setup.

Price Range: $25 - $200

- What is the name of the florist?
- What is the website and e-mail of the florist?
- What is the address of the florist?
- What are your business hours?
- What is the name and phone number of my contact person?
- How many years of professional floral experience do you have?
- What percentage of your business is dedicated to weddings?
- Do you have access to out-of-season flowers?
- Will you visit my wedding sites to make floral recommendations?
- Can you preserve my bridal bouquet?
- Do you rent vases and candleholders?
- Can you provide silk flowers?
- What is the cost of the desired bridal bouquet?
- What is the cost of the desired boutonniere?
- What is the cost of the desired corsage?
- Do you have liability insurance?
- What are your delivery/setup fees?
- What is your payment/cancellation policy?

FLOWERS AND THEIR SEASONS

POPULAR FLOWERS FOR A SUMMER BOUQUET

Allium	Pincushion
Amaryllis	Queen Anne's Lace
Billy Buttons	Saponaria
Celosia	Snapdragon
Dahlia	Speedwell
Delphinium	Sunflower
Liatris	Tuberose
Lisianthus	

POPULAR FLOWERS FOR A FALL BOUQUET

Amaryllis	Narcissus
Anemones	Protea
Dahlia	Snapdragon
Delphinium	Star of Bethlehem
Liatris	Tuberose
Lisianthus	

POPULAR FLOWERS FOR A WINTER BOUQUET

Amaryllis	Protea
Anemones	Star of Bethlehem
Narcissus	Tulip
	Waxflower

POPULAR FLOWERS FOR A SPRING BOUQUET

Allium	Narcissus
Anemones	Peony
Billy Buttons	Ranunculus
Celosia	Snapdragon
Daffodils	Sunflower
Liatris	Sweet Pea
Lily of the Valley	Tulip
Lisianthus	Waxflower

POPULAR FLOWERS YEAR-ROUND

Alstroemeria	Freesia
Aster	Gardenia
Baby's Breath	Gerbera Gladiolus
Bachelor's Button	Iris
Bird of Paradise	Lily Nerine
Bouvardia	Orchid
Calla Lily	Rose
Carnation	Statice
Chrysanthemum	Stephanotis
Eucalyptus	Stock

DECORATIONS

DECORATIONS CAN ENHANCE YOUR wedding by unifying all of the components of your ceremony and reception. Decorations can range anywhere from floral arrangements, twinkling lights, and centerpieces to more personal touches such as seating cards, menus, favors, and more. Most items, from stationery to place settings, are purchased or arranged based on a unified theme. For example, if the theme is Asian inspired, paper lanterns and take-out boxes can create beautiful "Japanese style" ambience.

TABLE CENTERPIECES

Each of the tables at your reception, including the head table, should be decorated with a centerpiece.

Options: Candles, mirrors, and flowers are popular choices for table centerpieces. However, the options are endless. Just be creative! An arrangement of shells, for example, makes a very nice centerpiece for a seaside reception. Votive candles set on top of a mirror make a romantic centerpiece for an evening reception.

A wreath of greenery woven with colored ribbon makes a delightful centerpiece. Use a different color ribbon at each table and have your guests seated according to ribbon color!

Things to Consider: Select a table centerpiece which complements your colors and/or setting. The centerpiece for the head table should be larger or more elaborate than the ones for the other tables. Make sure that your centerpiece is kept low enough so as not to hinder conversation among guests seated across from each other. Consider using a centerpiece that your guests can take home as a memento of your wedding.

Tips to Save Money: Make your own table centerpieces using materials that are not expensive.

Price Range: $10 - $100 each

BALLOONS

Balloons are often used to decorate a reception site. A popular idea is to release balloons at the church or reception. This adds a festive, exciting, and memorable touch to your wedding. Balloons can be used to create an arch backdrop for the wedding cake or inexpensive centerpieces for the tables.

Things to Consider: Color coordinate your balloons to match your color scheme. Choose colors from your bouquet or your bridesmaids' dresses. Balloons should be delivered and set up well in advance—at least before the photographer shows up.

If you are planning to release balloons at the church or reception, check with your city. Releasing balloons in some cities might be illegal. Also make sure there are no wires where balloons can get entangled. If they do, you could be held responsible for damages or clean-up expenses.

Tips to Save Money: Balloons are less expensive than fresh flowers and can be used as a substitute for flowers to decorate the reception site.

Price Range: $75 - $500

TRANSPORTATION

IT IS CUSTOMARY FOR THE BRIDE AND HER father to ride to the ceremony site together on the wedding day. You may also include some or all members of your wedding party. Normally a procession to the church begins with the bride's mother and several of the bride's attendants in the first vehicle. If desired, you can provide a second vehicle for the rest of the attendants. The bride and her father will go in the last vehicle. This vehicle will also be used to transport the bride and groom to the reception site after the ceremony.

TRANSPORTATION

Options: There are various options for transportation. The most popular choice is a limousine since it is big and open and can accommodate several people, as well as your bridal gown. You can also choose to rent a car that symbolizes your personality as a couple.

TRANSPORTATION

There are luxury cars such as Mercedes Benz, sports cars such as a Ferraris, and vintage vehicles such as 1950s Thunderbirds or 1930s Cadillacs. If your ceremony and reception sites are fairly close together, and if weather permits, you might want to consider a more romantic form of transportation, such as a horse-drawn carriage.

Things to Consider: In some areas of the country, limousines are booked on a three-hour minimum basis.

Beware: Make sure the company you choose is fully licensed and has liability insurance. Do not pay the full amount until after the event.

Tips to Save Money: Consider hiring only one large limousine. This limousine can transport you, your parents, and your attendants to the ceremony, and then you and your new husband from the ceremony to the reception.

Price Range: $35 - $100 per hour

- What is the name of the transportation service?
- What is the website and e-mail of the transportation service?
- What is the address of the transportation service?
- What is the name and phone number of my contact person?
- How many years have you been in business?
- How many vehicles do you have available?
- Can you provide a back-up vehicle in case of an emergency?
- What types of vehicles are available?
- What are the various sizes of vehicles available?
- How old are the vehicles?
- How many drivers are available?
- Can you show me photos of your drivers?
- How do your drivers dress for weddings?
- Do you have liability insurance?
- What is the minimum amount of time required to rent a vehicle?
- What is the cost per hour? Two hours? Three hours?
- How much gratuity is expected?
- What is your payment/cancellation policy?

RENTAL ITEMS

NOT ALL ITEMS NEED TO BE PURCHASED for the ceremony and reception. There are many items that you have the option of renting, such as a tent, canopy, chairs, and linens for the reception. This allows you to host a reception in your own home or in less traditional locations, such as an art museum, a local park, or at the beach. Be sure to take into account the cost for all these rental items when creating your budget.

BRIDAL SLIP

The bridal slip is an undergarment which gives the bridal gown its proper shape.

Things to Consider: Be sure to wear the same slip you'll be wearing on your wedding day during your fittings. Many bridal salons rent slips. Schedule an appointment to pick up your slip one week before the wedding; otherwise, you run the risk of not having one available on your wedding day. If rented, the slip will have to be returned shortly after the wedding. Arrange for someone to do this for you within the allotted time.

Tips to Save Money: Rent a slip rather than purchasing one; chances are you will never use it again.

Price Range: $25 - $75

CEREMONY ACCESSORIES

Ceremony rental accessories are the additional items needed for the ceremony but not included in the ceremony site fee.

Options: Ceremony rental accessories may include the following items:

Aisle Runner: A thin rug made of plastic, paper or cloth extending the length of the aisle. It is rolled out after the mothers are seated, just prior to the processional. Plastic or paper doesn't work well on grass; but if you must use one of these types of runners, make sure the grass is clipped short.

Kneeling Cushion: A small cushion or pillow placed in front of the altar where the bride and groom kneel for their wedding blessing.

Arch (Christian): A white lattice or brass arch where the bride and groom exchange their vows, often decorated with flowers and greenery.

Chuppah (Jewish): A canopy under which a Jewish ceremony is performed, symbolizing cohabitation and consummation.

You may also need to consider renting audio equipment, aisle stanchions, candelabra, candles, candle-lighters, chairs, heaters, a gift table, a guest book stand, and a canopy.

Things to Consider: If you plan to rent any accessories for your ceremony, make sure the rental supplier has been in business for a reasonable period of time and has a good reputation. Reserve the items you need well in advance. Find out the company's payment, reservation, and cancellation policies.

Some companies allow you to reserve emergency items, such as heaters or canopies, without having to pay for them unless needed, in which case you would need to call the rental company a day or two in advance to request the items. If someone else requests the items you have reserved, the company should give you the right of first refusal.

Tips to Save Money: When considering a ceremony outside of a church, figure the cost of rental items. Negotiate a package deal, if possible, by renting items for both the ceremony and the reception from the same supplier. Consider renting these items from your florist so you only have to pay one delivery fee.

Price Range: $100 - $500

TENT/CANOPY

A large tent or canopy may be required for receptions held outdoors to protect you and your guests from the sun or rain. Usually rented through party rental suppliers, tents and canopies can be expensive due to the labor involved in delivery and setup.

Options: Tents and canopies come in different sizes and colors. Depending on the shape of your reception area, you may need to rent several smaller canopies rather than one large one. Contact several party rental suppliers to discuss the options.

Things to Consider: Consider this cost when making a decision between an outdoor and an indoor reception. In cooler weather, heaters may also be necessary.

Tips to Save Money: Shop early and compare prices with several party rental suppliers.

Price Range: $300 - $5,000

DANCE FLOOR

A dance floor will be provided by most hotels and clubs. However, if your reception site does not have a dance floor, you may need to rent one through your caterer or a party rental supplier.

Things to Consider: When comparing prices of dance floors, include the delivery and setup fees.

Price Range: $100 - $600

TABLES/CHAIRS

You will have to provide tables and chairs for your guests if your reception site or caterer doesn't provide them as part of their package. For a full meal, you will have to provide tables and seating for all guests. For a cocktail reception, you only need to provide tables and chairs for approximately 30 to 50 percent of your guests. Ask your caterer or reception site manager for advice.

Options: There are various types of tables and chairs to choose from. The most commonly used chairs for wedding receptions are typically white wooden or plastic chairs. The most common tables for receptions are round tables that seat eight guests. The most common head table arrangement is several rectangular tables placed end-to-end to seat your entire wedding party on one side, facing your guests. Contact various party rental suppliers to find out what types of chairs and tables they carry, as well as their price ranges.

Things to Consider: When comparing prices of renting tables and chairs, include the cost of delivery and setup.

Tips to Save Money: Attempt to negotiate free delivery and setup with party rental suppliers in exchange for giving them your business.

Price Range: $3 - $10 per person

LINEN/TABLEWARE

You will also need to provide linens and tableware for your reception if your reception site or caterer does not provide them as part of their package.

Options: For a sit-down reception where the meal is served by waiters and waitresses, tables are usually set with a cloth (usually white, but may be color coordinated with the wedding), a centerpiece, and complete place settings. At a less formal buffet reception where guests serve themselves, tables are covered with a cloth, but place settings are not mandatory. The necessary plates and silverware may be located at the buffet table, next to the food.

Things to Consider: Linens and tableware depend on the formality of your reception. When comparing prices of linens and tableware, include the cost of delivery and setup.

Price Range: $3 - $25 per person

- Holds the bride's ring for the groom, if no ring bearer, until needed by officiant.
- Witnesses the signing of the marriage license.
- Drives newlyweds to reception, if no hired driver.
- Offers first toast at reception, usually before dinner.
- Keeps groom on schedule.
- Dances with maid of honor during the bridal party dance.
- May drive couple to airport or honeymoon suite.
- Oversees return of tuxedo rentals for groom and ushers, on time and in good condition.

BRIDESMAIDS

- Assist maid of honor in planning bridal shower.
- Assist bride with errands and addressing invitations.
- Participate in all pre-wedding parties.
- Arrive at dressing site two hours before ceremony.
- Arrive dressed at ceremony site one hour before the wedding for photographs.
- Walk behind ushers in order of height during the processional, either in pairs or in single file.
- Sit next to ushers at the head table.
- Dance with ushers and other important guests.
- Encourage single women to participate in the bouquet-tossing ceremony.

USHERS

- Help best man with bachelor party.

WEDDING PARTY RESPONSIBILITIES

- Arrive dressed at ceremony site one hour before the wedding for photographs.
- Distribute wedding programs and maps to the reception as guests arrive.
- Seat guests at the ceremony as follows:
  - If female, offer the right arm.
  - If male, walk along his left side.
  - If couple, offer right arm to female; male follows a step or two behind.
  - Seat bride's guests in left pews.
  - Seat groom's guests in right pews.
  - Maintain equal number of guests in left and right pews, if possible.
  - If a group of guests arrive at the same time, seat the eldest woman first.
  - Just prior to the processional, escort groom's mother to her seat; then escort bride's mother to her seat.
- Two ushers may roll carpet down the aisle after both mothers are seated.
- If pew ribbons are used, two ushers may loosen them one row at a time after the ceremony.
- Direct guests to the reception site.
- Dance with bridesmaids and other important guests.

BRIDE'S MOTHER

- Helps prepare guest list for bride and her family.
- Helps plan the wedding ceremony and reception.
- Helps bride select her bridal gown.
- Helps bride keep track of gifts received.

- Selects her own attire according to the formality and color of the wedding.
- Makes accommodations for bride's out-of-town guests.
- Arrives dressed at ceremony site one hour before the wedding for photographs.
- Is the last person to be seated right before the processional begins.
- Sits in the left front pew to the left of bride's father during the ceremony.
- May stand up to signal the start of the processional.
- Can witness the signing of the marriage license.
- Dances with the groom after the first dance.
- Acts as hostess at the reception.

BRIDE'S FATHER

- Helps prepare guest list for bride and her family.
- Selects attire that complements groom's attire.
- Rides to the ceremony with bride in limousine.
- Arrives dressed at ceremony site one hour before the wedding for photographs.
- After giving bride away, sits in the left front pew to the right of bride's mother. If divorced, sits in second or third row unless financing the wedding.
- When officiant asks, "Who gives this bride away?" answers, "Her mother and I do," or something similar.
- Can witness the signing of the marriage license.
- Dances with bride after first dance.
- Acts as host at the reception.

WEDDING PARTY RESPONSIBILITIES

GROOM'S MOTHER

- Helps prepare guest list for groom and his family.
- Selects attire that complements mother of the bride's attire.
- Makes accommodations for groom's out-of-town guests.
- With groom's father, plans rehearsal dinner.
- Arrives dressed at ceremony site one hour before the wedding for photographs.
- May stand up to signal the start of the processional.
- Can witness the signing of the marriage license.

GROOM'S FATHER

- Helps prepare guest list for groom and his family.
- Selects attire that complements groom's attire.
- With groom's mother, plans rehearsal dinner.
- Offers toast to bride at rehearsal dinner.
- Arrives dressed at ceremony site one hour before the wedding for photographs.
- Can witness the signing of the marriage license.

FLOWER GIRL

- Usually between the ages of four and eight.
- Attends rehearsal to practice, but is not required to attend pre-wedding parties.
- Arrives dressed at ceremony site 45 minutes before the wedding for photos.

- Carries a basket filled with loose rose petals to strew along bride's path during processional, if allowed by ceremony site.
- If very young, may sit with her parents during ceremony.

RING BEARER

- Usually between the ages of four and eight.
- Attends rehearsal to practice but is not required to attend pre-wedding parties.
- Arrives at ceremony site 45 minutes before the wedding for photographs.
- Carries a white pillow with rings attached.
- If younger than seven years, carries mock rings.
- If very young, may sit with his parents during ceremony.
- If mock rings are used, turns the ring pillow over at the end of the ceremony.

WHO PAYS
FOR WHAT

BRIDE AND/OR BRIDE'S FAMILY

- Engagement party
- Wedding consultant's fee
- Bridal gown, veil, and accessories
- Wedding stationery, calligraphy, and postage
- Wedding gift for bridal couple
- Groom's wedding ring
- Gifts for bridesmaids
- Bridesmaids' bouquets
- Pre-wedding parties and bridesmaids' luncheon
- Photography and videography
- Bride's medical exam and blood test
- Wedding guest book and other accessories
- Total cost of the ceremony, including location, flowers, music, rental items, and accessories
- Total cost of the reception, including location, flowers, music, rental items, accessories, food,

beverages, cake, decorations, favors, etc.
- Transportation for bridal party to ceremony and reception
- Own attire and travel expenses

GROOM AND/OR GROOM'S FAMILY

- Own travel expenses and attire
- Rehearsal dinner
- Wedding gift for bridal couple
- Bride's wedding ring
- Gifts for groom's attendants
- Medical exam for groom including blood test
- Bride's bouquet and going away corsage
- Mothers' and grandmothers' corsages
- All boutonnieres
- Officiant's fee
- Marriage license
- Honeymoon expenses

ATTENDANTS

- Own attire except flowers
- Travel expenses
- Bridal shower paid for by maid of honor and bridesmaids
- Bachelor party paid for by best man and ushers

WEDDING
FORMATIONS

THE FOLLOWING SECTION ILLUSTRATES THE typical ceremony formations (processional, recessional, and altar lineup) for both Christian and Jewish weddings, as well as the typical formations for the receiving line, head table, and parents' tables at the reception.

These ceremony formations are included in the Wedding Party Responsibility Cards, published by WS Publishing Group. This attractive set of cards makes it very easy for members of your wedding party to remember their place in these formations. Give one card to each member of your wedding party ... they will appreciate it. This book of cards is available at most major bookstores.

𝒜LTAR ℒINE 𝒰P

Bride's Pews   Groom's Pews

ABBREVIATIONS

B=Bride
G=Groom
BM=Best Man
MH=Maid of Honor
BF=Bride's Father
BMo=Bride's Mother
O=Officiant

GF=Groom's Father
GM=Groom's Mother
BMa=Bridesmaids
U=Ushers
FG=Flower Girl
RB=Ring Bearer

$\mathscr{P}$ROCESSIONAL $\mathscr{R}$ECESSIONAL

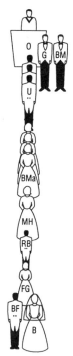
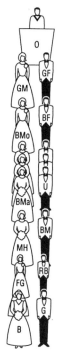

ABBREVIATIONS

B=Bride
G=Groom
BM=Best Man
MH=Maid of Honor
BF=Bride's Father
BMo=Bride's Mother
O=Officiant

GF=Groom's Father
GM=Groom's Mother
BMa=Bridesmaids
U=Ushers
FG=Flower Girl
RB=Ring Bearer

𝒜LTAR ℒINE 𝒰P

Groom's Pews   Bride's Pews

ABBREVIATIONS

B=Bride	GF=Groom's Father
G=Groom	GM=Groom's Mother
BM=Best Man	BMa=Bridesmaids
MH=Maid of Honor	U=Ushers
BF=Bride's Father	FG=Flower Girl
BMo=Bride's Mother	RB=Ring Bearer
O=Officiant	

𝒫ROCESSIONAL   ℛECESSIONAL

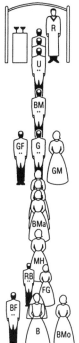 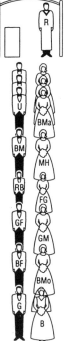

ABBREVIATIONS

B=Bride
G=Groom
BM=Best Man
MH=Maid of Honor
BF=Bride's Father
BMo=Bride's Mother
O=Officiant

GF=Groom's Father
GM=Groom's Mother
BMa=Bridesmaids
U=Ushers
FG=Flower Girl
RB=Ring Bearer

$\mathscr{R}$ECEIVING $\mathscr{L}$INE

BMo BF GM GF B G MH BMa BMa BMa

$\mathscr{H}$EAD $\mathscr{T}$ABLE

BMa U BMa BM B G MH U BMa U

$\mathscr{P}$ARENTS' $\mathscr{T}$ABLE

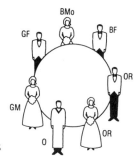

ABBREVIATIONS

B=Bride
G=Groom
BM=Best Man
MH=Maid of Honor
BF=Bride's Father
BMo=Bride's Mother
O=Officiant

GF=Groom's Father
GM=Groom's Mother
BMa=Bridesmaids
U=Ushers
FG=Flower Girl
RB=Ring Bearer

THINGS TO BRING

TO THE REHEARSAL

BRIDE'S LIST

- ❏ Wedding announcements
  (give to maid of honor to mail after wedding)
- ❏ Bridesmaids' gifts (if not already given)
- ❏ Camera and film
- ❏ Fake bouquet or ribbon bouquet from bridal shower
- ❏ Groom's gift (if not already given)
- ❏ Reception maps and wedding programs
- ❏ Rehearsal information and ceremony formations
- ❏ Flower girl basket and ring bearer pillow
- ❏ Seating diagrams for head table and parents' tables
- ❏ Wedding schedule of events/timeline
- ❏ Tape/CD player with wedding music

THINGS TO BRING

GROOM'S LIST

- ❑ Bride's gift (if not already given)
- ❑ Marriage license
- ❑ Ushers' gifts (if not already given)
- ❑ Service providers' fees to give to best man or wedding consultant so s/he can pay them at the wedding

TO THE CEREMONY

BRIDE'S LIST

- ❑ Aspirin/Alka Seltzer
- ❑ Bobby pins
- ❑ Breath spray/mints
- ❑ Bridal gown
- ❑ Bridal gown box
- ❑ Cake knife
- ❑ Going away clothes
- ❑ Clear nail polish
- ❑ Deodorant
- ❑ Garter
- ❑ Gloves
- ❑ Groom's ring
- ❑ Guest book
- ❑ Hairbrush
- ❑ Hair spray
- ❑ Headpiece
- ❑ Iron
- ❑ Jewelry
- ❑ Kleenex
- ❑ Lint brush
- ❑ Luggage
- ❑ Makeup
- ❑ Mirror
- ❑ Nail polish
- ❑ Panty hose
- ❑ Passport
- ❑ Perfume
- ❑ Personal camera

- Plume pen for guest book
- Powder
- Purse
- Safety pins
- Scotch tape/masking tape
- Sewing kit
- Shoes
- Something old
- Something new
- Something borrowed
- Something blue
- Sixpence for shoe
- Spot remover
- Straight pins
- Tampons or sanitary napkins
- Toasting goblets
- Toothbrush and paste

GROOM'S LIST

- Airline tickets
- Announcements
- Aspirin/Alka Seltzer
- Breath spray/mints
- Bride's ring
- Going away clothes
- Cologne
- Cuff Links
- Cummerbund
- Deodorant
- Hair comb
- Hair product
- Kleenex
- Lint brush
- Luggage
- Neck tie
- Passport
- Shirt
- Shoes
- Socks
- Toothbrush and paste
- Tuxedo
- Underwear

EASY HONEYMOON PLANNING

A comprehensive guide containing
all the information a bride and groom should
know when planning a honeymoon.

HONEYMOONS

YOUR HONEYMOON IS THE TIME TO celebrate your new life together as a married couple. It should be the vacation of a lifetime. This does not necessarily mean spending your life's earnings, but the vacation should reflect the special interests you share as a couple.

The honeymoon is traditionally the groom's responsibility. However, the planning of your honeymoon should be a joint decision as to where to go, how long to stay, and how much money to spend.

You will find many tools and suggestions on the following pages to help you plan this important trip. After reading this book, you will have information on different types of honeymoons, and you should be able to determine the perfect honeymoon destination, research and select a responsible travel agent, gather useful information using the resource leads provided, establish a reasonable budget with confidence, and—most importantly—walk away with the assurance that you are planning the honeymoon of a lifetime! Start planning your honeymoon months before the wedding. Many locations that are popular with honeymooners tend to book fairly quickly, so the earlier you plan your trip, the better values you'll usually find.

There are many choices to make and many plans to be made, but most of them seem to fall into place once you've made the toughest decision ... where to go.

Many people have a preconceived notion of where a honeymoon should take place. Indeed, year after year these locations are some of the places most frequently visited by newlyweds. We'll take a look at some of these "traditional" destinations as well as some that are a little less traditional.

Think about what you and your fiancé might find appealing (and unappealing) in the following honeymoon vacations. Be careful not to assume what your new spouse may be looking for in a honeymoon. Couples are often surprised when they discover what the other partner considers a "vacation." Refer to the section entitled Choosing a Destination to determine what each other's ideal vacation includes.

TYPES OF HONEYMOONS

Listed on the following pages are sample honeymoon plans—both traditional and less traditional. A brief description of some of the most popular honeymoon trips (ones that have remained popular with newlyweds for generations) is provided as well.

You can get very helpful information on planning a vacation package in the following brochures from the United States Tour Operator Association, (212) 599-6599, www.ustoa. com.

- How to Select a Tour Vacation Package
- Worldwide Tour and Vacation Package Finder
- The Standard for Confident Travel

TRADITIONAL HONEYMOONS

CRUISES

Cruises are a popular retreat for those who want the luxury of a hospitable resort with the added benefit of visiting one or more new areas. There are hundreds of different cruise options available to you. Typically, almost everything is included in the cost of your cruise: extravagant dining, unlimited group and individual activities, relaxing days and lively nights.

Costs vary greatly depending on the location the cruise will visit (if any) and your cabin accommodations. Locations range from traveling the Mississippi River to circling the Greek Isles. Spend some time choosing your cabin. Most of them are small, but pay attention to distracting things, such as noisy areas and busy pathways, that might be located close by.

Even though most everything is included in your cost, be sure to ask about those items which may not be included. Alcoholic beverages, sundries, spa treatments and tips generally are not included. Request a helpful publication entitled Answers to Your Most Frequently Asked Questions, published by Cruise Lines International Association, (212) 921-0066, www.cruising.org.

ALL-INCLUSIVE RESORTS

Many newlyweds, tired from the previous months of wedding planning and accompanying stress, opt for the worry-free guarantee of an all-inclusive resort. Some resorts are for the entire family, some are for couples only (not necessarily newlywed), and some are strictly for honeymooners. Most of these resorts are nestled on a picturesque island beach catering to your relaxation needs.

Most offer numerous sports, water activities, entertainment, and exceptional service and attention. Your costs will vary depending on the location you choose, and there are many to choose from. "All-inclusive" means everything is included in your price. You won't have to worry about meals, drinks, tour fees or even tips.

One way of considering if this is a good option for you is to list all of the activities that the vacation package offers that you are interested in. Add up the individual costs and compare. If you wouldn't be participating much in the activities, food, and drink, you may actually save money by arranging your own trip at an independent resort. Even still, many couples prefer to spend the extra money in exchange for a vacation free of planning and wearying decisions.

Because of its convenience, many couples choose this resort option as the setting for their honeymoon. Some of the most popular all-inclusive resorts are Sandals and Club Med.

THE POCONOS

The Poconos Honeymoon resorts are located in Pennsylvania and are considered to be some of the most popular honeymoon destinations around. The Poconos offer a variety of individual resorts, each heavily laden with fanciful symbols of romance and sweet desires. The atmosphere is perfect for those who want to be enveloped in a surrounding where you'll never forget you're in love and on your honeymoon. Some travel packages here are considered all-inclusive, but as always, be sure to ask about exclusions and extras. For information about honeymooning in the Poconos, call 1-800-POCONOS.

WALT DISNEY WORLD

Another popular destination for those seeking a "theme" resort are those offered as Disney's Fairy Tale Honeymoons.

These vacation packages include accommodations at Disney's exclusive resorts and admission to their theme parks. Some packages are also available with accommodations at some of the privately owned resorts at Disney World. Prices for Disney packages can range greatly depending on your tastes and the amount of activity you desire. For information on Disney's honeymoon packages, call (407) 828-3400 or visit them online at www.disneyweddings.com.

Inquire with your travel agent about day or overnight cruises leaving from nearby ports in Florida. This is one way to combine two very popular honeymoon options into one!

OTHER POPULAR AND TRADITIONAL HONEYMOON PLANS ARE AS FOLLOWS

- Enjoying the beaches and unique treasures of the Hawaiian islands

- Exploring Northern California's romantic wine country

- Ski and snowboard package getaways in Vermont, New Hampshire, Colorado, and Northern California

- Camping and hiking within the beautiful and adventurous National Parks

- Sightseeing, touring, and exploring a variety of points in Europe via the rail system

- Island hopping on a cruise ship around the Greek Isles

- Enjoying a fanciful and adventurous journey on the Orient Express

LESS TRADITIONAL HONEYMOONS

- Bicycling in Nova Scotia while relaxing at quaint bed and breakfast inns

- Participating in a white water river rafting expedition

- Mingling with the owners and fellow guests on an Old West dude ranch

- Visiting landmarks and parks while enjoying the convenience of a traveling home in a rented RV

- Mustering up the courage and stamina for an aggressive hiking tour of the Canadian Rockies

- Training for and participating in a dog sled race in the brisk tundra of Alaska

- "Roughing it" while enjoying the splendor of a safari in East Africa

CHOOSING YOUR DESTINATION

MAYBE YOUR IDEA OF A PERFECT honeymoon is ten days of adventure and discovery; but for your fiancé, it may be ten days of resting in a beach chair and romantic strolls in the evening. The choices for honeymoon vacations are as varied as the bride and groom themselves. Deciding together on a honeymoon destination is a wonderful opportunity to discover more about each other and negotiate a vacation that will leave both of you relaxed, fulfilled, and even more in love.

First, determine the type of atmosphere and climate you prefer. Then consider the types of activities you would like to engage in.

Do you want the weather to be hot for swimming at the beach ... or warm for long guided tours of unknown cities ... or cooler for daylong hikes in the woods ... or cold for optimum skiing conditions? Keep in mind the time of year in which your wedding falls. Will you be escaping from extreme temperatures?

CHOOSING YOUR DESTINATION

If you have a specific destination in mind, you (or your travel agent) will need to do some research to be sure the weather conditions will be suitable for your planned activities.

Review the previous chapters on traditional and nontraditional honeymoons and note what you feel are the pros and cons of each type of vacation. The two of you should have lots of images and possibilities in your mind at this point! The next step is to determine the most perfect atmosphere to provide the setting for your honeymoon. The following sections, "Creating a Wish List" and "Helpful Resources," will guide you through this next step and beyond.

CREATING A WISH LIST

Together with your fiancé, complete the wish list worksheet on pages 296 through 300. You should each check off your preferences, even if both of you don't agree on them. There are many locations that provide a variety of activities. Remember, you don't need to spend every minute of your honeymoon together, but your honeymoon destination should be one that intrigues both of you.

This worksheet is divided into 5 sections. You will be considering location, accommodations, meals, activities, and nightlife. While completing the worksheet, be as true to your interests as possible; don't concern yourself with finances and practicality at this point. This is your chance to let your mind wander! Think about what you would like to fill your days and nights with. This is the honeymoon of your dreams.

CHOOSING YOUR DESTINATION

You step out of the plane, train, car or boat that took you to your honeymoon destination. You sigh with satisfaction at the memory of your flawless and enjoyable wedding as your feet touch the ground.

What type of overall atmosphere do you see yourself stepping into? What is the weather like?

Do you picture a long stretch of beach, towering mountains, blossoming vineyards, or city skyscrapers? Is the dry sand of the desert blowing, or is everything captured under glistening snow caps?

Are there many people walking around (many locals, many tourists), or is it a secluded retreat?

Are you relaxing indoors in a resort with a pampering environment that caters to your comfort, or do you return to a simple, modest hotel or motel after a long day of sightseeing, touring, and dining? Are you camping in the middle of your activities—hiking, climbing, fishing, etc.?

Do you see yourself interacting much with others? Would you like to have these activities be organized? Are there vistas and horizons to gaze endlessly upon, or is there an abundance of visual activity and changing scenery?

Are you enjoying exotic foods elaborately displayed and available to you at your leisure? Are you testing out your sense of adventure on the local cuisine and dining hot spots? Are you eating fast foods and pizza in exchange for spending your time and money on other items and activities that make your vacation exciting?

Are your evenings filled with romantic strolls or festivities that run late into the night? Are you staying in for romantic evenings or re-energizing for another busy day of honeymooning?

HOW TO USE THIS WORKSHEET

Each of you separately should place a check mark next to the items or images on the wish list that appeal to you. After you have finished, highlight those items that both of you feel are important (the items that were checked by both of you).

Next, each of you should highlight, in a different colored marker or pen, 2-3 items in each category that you feel are very important to you individually (even though the other person may not have checked it.

Your wish lists, after completing this exercise, will probably look like a list of all of the positive elements of all of your dream vacations combined. This is good; you should list as many things as you can think of. The more information you have, the better the suggestions your travel agent (or yourself if you'll be doing your own research) will be able to make.

Together, using this wish list, you will discover a honeymoon destination and match a honeymoon style that will fulfill your dreams. The resource leads and exercises provided in the rest of this book will help you get from wish list to reality. Happy planning!

LOCATION

	Bride	Groom
Hot Weather		
Mild Weather		
Cold Weather		
Dry Climate		
Moist Climate		
Sand and Beaches		
Lakes/Ponds		
Wilderness/Wooded Area		
Mountains		
Fields		
City Streets		
Small Local Town		
Large Metropolitan Area		
Popular Tourist Destination		
Visiting Among the Locals		
Nighttime Weather Conducive to Outdoor Activities		
Nighttime Weather Conducive to Indoor Activities		
"Modern" Resources and Service Available		
"Roughing It" On Your Own		
Culture and Customs You Are Familiar and Comfortable With		
New Cultures and Customs You Would Like to Get to Know		

ACCOMMODATIONS

	Bride	Groom
Part of a Larger Resort Community		
A Stand-Alone Building		
Lodging Amongst Other Fellow Tourists		
Lodging Amongst Couples Only		
Lodging Amongst Fellow Newlyweds Only		
Lodging Amongst Locals		
Large Room or Suite		
Plush, Highly Decorated Surroundings		
Modestly Sized Room		
Modest Décor		
Balcony		
Private Jacuzzi in Room		
Room Service		
Chamber Maid Service		
Laundry/Dry Cleaning Service Available		
Laundry Room Available		
Beauty Salon on Premises		
Gym on Premises		
Gift Shop on Premises		
Pool on Premises		
Poolside Bar Service		
Sauna, Hot Tub on Premises		
Common Gathering Lounge for Guests		

MEALS

	Bride	Groom
Casual Dining		
Formal Dining		
Prepared by Executive Chefs		
Prepared by Yourself/Grocery Store		
Variety of Local and Regional Cuisine		
Traditional American Cuisine		
Opportunity for Picnics		
Exotic, International Menu		
Entertainment While Dining		
Planned Meal Times		
Dining Based on Your Own Schedule		
Fast Food Restaurants		
Vegetarian/Special Diet Meals		
Delis, Diners		

ACTIVITIES

	Bride	Groom
Sunbathing		
Snorkeling		
Diving		
Swimming		
Jet Skiing		
Water Skiing		
Fishing		
Sailing		

ACTIVITIES

	Bride	Groom
Snow Skiing		
Snowboarding		
Hiking/Rock Climbing		
Camping		
Golf		
Tennis		
Aerobics		
Sight-seeing Suggestions and Guidance		
Planned Bus/Guided Tours		
Ability to Go Off on Your Own		
Historic Tours		
Art Museums		
Theater		
Exploring Family Heritage		

NIGHTLIFE

	Bride	Groom
Nightlife		
Quiet Strolls		
Outdoor Activities		
Sitting and Relaxing Outdoors		
Sitting and Relaxing in Front of a Fireplace		
Being Alone with Each Other		
Being Out with the Locals		

NIGHTLIFE

	Bride	Groom
Being Out with Other Newlyweds		
Discovering New Cultures and Forms of Entertainment		
Dancing		
Visiting Bars/Pubs		
Theater/Shows		
Gambling		

OTHER IMPORTANT ELEMENTS

	Bride	Groom

CREATING A WISH LIST

Now that you have created a wish list, take this list to your travel agent. If you don't already have a travel agent, use the following section to select a reputable agent.

A good travel agent, especially one who works with a lot of honeymooners, will be able to tell you about several different places that match your wish list while staying within your budget. (The section entitled Creating a Budget will prove invaluable in determining exactly what your budget will be.) Your travel agent should be able to provide a variety of options which contain different combinations of the elements of your wish list. Discuss with him or her which "lower priority" items you are willing to forego in order to experience the best of your "top priorities."

HELPFUL RESOURCES

THE FOLLOWING PAGES INCLUDE helpful resources that will come in handy when planning your honeymoon. Find information regarding travel agents and guidebooks, as well as websites and telephone numbers of travel bureaus from around the world.

TRAVEL AGENTS

Using the services of a good travel agent will take a lot of unnecessary pressure off of you. In the past, you may have felt you did not need the assistance of a travel agent when planning a vacation. Planning a honeymoon, however, can often be far more involved and stressful than a "regular" vacation, due to the simple fact that you are also deeply enmeshed in the planning of your wedding!

Therefore, you should take advantage of the professional

HELPFUL RESOURCES

resources available to you when working out the small details and finding the best values. Keep in mind, though, that you will still probably want to do some research on your own, ask for second opinions and, most of all, read the fine print.

Since a travel agent can become one of your most valuable resources, you will want to consider a few important things when trying to select one. Ask family, friends, and coworkers for personal recommendations (especially from former honeymooners). If you are unable to find an agent through a personal referral, then select a few agencies that are established nearby from newspapers, phone books, etc.

Next, you will want to make an appointment with an agent or speak to one over the phone. Pay close attention to the following and then make your decision.

Find out if they are a member of the American Society of Travel Agents (ASTA). Additionally, find out if they are also a Certified Travel Counselor (CTC), or possibly a Destination Specialist (DS).

ASTA: Members of this organization are required to have at least 5 years of travel agent experience. They also agree to adhere to strict codes and standards of integrity in travel issues as established by the national society. In most states, there are no formal regulations requiring certain qualifications for being a travel agent. In other words, any person can decide to call him/herself a travel agent.

CTC: Certified Travel Counselors have successfully completed a 2-year program in travel management.

DS: Destination Specialists have successfully completed studies focusing on a particular region of travel.

For a list of ASTA agencies in your area, call or write:

> American Society of Travel Agents
> Consumer Affairs Department
> 1101 King Street, Suite 200
> Alexandria, VA 22314
> (703) 739-2782
> www.ASTAnet.com

For a list of Destination Specialists and Certified Travel Agents in your area, call or write:

> Institute of Certified Travel Agents
> 148 Linden Street
> P.O. Box 56
> Wellesley, MA 02181
> (800) 542-4282
> *(press "0" to be connected to a Travel Counselor)*
> www.ICTA.com

QUESTIONS TO QUALIFY YOUR TRAVEL AGENT:

- How long has the travel agency been in business?

- How long has the travel agent been with the agency?

- How much experience does the travel agent have? Any special studies or travels?

- Do they have a good resource library?

- Does the agent/agency have a variety of brochures to offer?

- Do they have travel videos to lend?

- Do they have a recommended reading list of travel aid books?

- Does the agent seem to understand your responses on your wish list and budget?

- Does he/she seem excited to help you?

- Does the agent listen carefully to your ideas? Take notes on your conversations? Ask you questions to ensure a full understanding?

- Is the agent able to offer a variety of different possibilities that suit your interests based on your wish list? Do the suggestions fall within your budget?

- Can the agent relay back to you (in his/her own words) what your wish list priorities are and what your budget priorities are?

- Is the agent prompt in getting back in touch with you?

- Is the agent reasonably quick in coming up with suggestions and alternatives? Are the suggestions exciting and within reason?

- Does the agent take notes on your interests (degree of sports, leisure, food, etc.)?

- Does the travel agency provide a 24 hour emergency help line?

- Are you documenting your conversations and getting all of your travel plans and reservations confirmed in writing?

Aside from just offering information and arrangements about locations and discounts, a good travel agent should also provide you with information about passports, customs, travel and health insurance, travelers' checks, and any other information important to a traveler.

OTHER SOURCES

National bridal magazines and general travel magazines are a great place to search for honeymoon ideas. But remember, you cannot always believe every word in paid advertising.

HELPFUL RESOURCES

In addition to the information your travel agent provides, you can also obtain maps, brochures, and other useful items on your own. At the end of this section, you will find many useful phone numbers to help you in contacting tourist bureaus and travel agencies worldwide. These offices are extremely helpful in acquiring both general information (about weather, tourist attractions, landmarks, and even coupons or promotional brochures "selling" the area) and more specific information about reputable hotels, inns, bed and breakfasts, restaurants, etc.

Also provided in this section are phone numbers for sources specializing in information about traveling by train (in the United States as well as abroad) and for camping and hiking throughout the country.

The internet, your local library, the travel section of book stores, and travel stores are excellent sources for finding information and tips relevant to your travel needs. You will find books on traveling in general as well as books specific to the region or destination you will be visiting. There are numerous tour books, maps, language books and tapes, as well as books about a location's culture, traditions, customs, climate, and geography.

These books are a great source of information since they are independent from the locations they describe and are therefore impartial, objective, and usually contain correct, unbiased information. You can also find books and other resources describing (and sometimes rating) restaurants, hotels, shows, and tours. Books on bargain hunting and finding the best deals are common as well.

SOURCES TO READ

- *The Ultimate Guide to the World's Best Wedding and Honeymoon Destinations*, written by Elizabeth & Alex Lluch. A comprehensive resource for planning your honeymoon, including information on popular destinations and information on hotels and resorts.

- The Stephen Birnbaum travel guides

- Frommer's guides

- Michelin Green Guides; Michelin Red Guides

- Insight Guides

- Let's Go! guides

- Fodor's guides

- Fielding's travel books

- *The New York Times Practical Traveler*

- *Mobil Travel Guide*

BACKGROUND NOTES

- National Park Service Publications
  (202) 208-4747
  www.nps.gov

- National Forest Service Publications
  (202) 205-8333
  A Guide to Your National Forests
  www.fs.fed.us

STATE TOURISM BUREAUS

Alabama Bureau of Tourism
800-ALABAMA
www.touralabama.com

Alaska Travel Industry Association

907-929-2200
www.travelalaska.com

Arizona Office of Tourism
866-275-5816
www.arizonaguide.com

**Arkansas Dept. of Parks
and Tourism**
800-NATURAL
www.arkansas.com

California Tourism Office
800-862-2543
www.gocalif.com

Colorado Tourism Board
800-COLORADO
www.colorado.com

Connecticut Vacation Center
800-CT-BOUND
www.ctbound.com

**D.C. Convention
and Visitors Association**
202-789-7000
www.washington.org

Delaware Tourism Office
866-284-7483
www.visitdelaware.com

Visit Florida
850-488-5607
www.flausa.com

**Georgia Department of
Industry Trade**
800-VISIT-GA
www.georgia.org

**Hawaii Visitors &
Convention Bureau**
800-464-2924
www.hawaii.com

**Idaho Division of Tourism
Development**
800-635-7820
www.visitid.org

Illinois Bureau of Tourism
800-2-CONNECT
www.enjoyillinois.com

**Indiana Department
of Commerce**
888-ENJOY-IN
www.enjoyindiana.com

Iowa Tourism Office
888-472-6035
www.traveliowa.com

**Kansas Department of
Travel & Tourism**
800-2-KANSAS
www.travelks.com

**Kentucky Dept. of Travel
Development**
800-225-TRIP
www.kentuckytourism.com

Louisiana Office of Tourism
800-33-GUMBO
www.louisianatravel.com

Maine Bureau of Tourism
888-624-6345
www.visitmaine.com

**Maryland Office of Tourist
Development**
800-MD-IS-FUN
www.mdisfun.org

**Massachusetts Department
of Tourism**
800-447-MASS
www.massvacation.com

**Michigan Department
of Commerce**
888-78-GREAT
www.michigan.org

Minnesota Office of Tourism
800-657-3700
www.exploreminnesota.com

Mississippi Office of Tourism
800-WARMEST
www.visitmississippi.org

Missouri Travel Center
800-877-1234
www.visitmo.com

**Montana Travel Promotion
Division**
800-VISIT-MT
www.visitmt.com

**Nebraska Dept. of Travel
and Tourism**
800-228-4307
www.visitnebraska.org

Nevada Commission
on Tourism
800-NEVADA-8
www.travelnevada.com

New Hampshire
Division of Tourism
800-FUN-IN-NH
www.visitnh.gov

New Jersey Office of
Travel & Tourism
800-JERSEY-7
www.visitnj.org

New Mexico
Department of Tourism
800-SEE-NEWMEX
www.newmexico.org

New York Division
of Tourism
800-CALL-NYS
www.www.iloveny.com

North Carolina Travel
& Tourism Division
800-VISIT-NC
www.visitnc.com

North Dakota
Tourism Division
800-HELLO-ND
www.ndtourism.com

Ohio Department of
Travel & Tourism
800-BUCKEYE
www.ohiotourism.com

Oklahoma Tourism and
Recreation Dept.
800-652-6552
www.travelok.com

Oregon Tourism Commission
800-547-7842
www.traveloregon.com

Pennsylvania Department
of Tourism
800-VISIT-PA
www.experiencepa.com

Rhode Island Tourism Division
800-556-2484
www.visitrhodeisland.com

South Carolina Dept. of Parks,
Recreation and Tourism
800-346-3634
www.discoversouthcarolina.com

South Dakota Division
of Tourism
800-S-DAKOTA
www.travelsd.com

HELPFUL RESOURCES

Tennessee Department
of Tourism
800-GO-2-TENN
www.tnvacation.com

Texas Travel and
Information Bureau
800-888-8-TEX
www.traveltex.com

Utah Travel Council
800-200-1160
www.utah.com

Vermont Travel Division
800-VERMONT
www.travel-vermont.com

Virginia Division of Tourism
800-VISIT-VA
www.virginia.org

Washington Tourism Development
800-544-1800
www.experiencewashington.com

West Virginia Div. of
Tourism & Parks
800-CALL-WVA
www.callwva.com

Wisconsin Division of Tourism
800-432-TRIP
www.travelwisconsin.com

Wyoming Travel & Tourism
800-CALL-WYO
www.wyomingtourism.org

U.S. Virgin Islands
Division of Tourism
www.usvitourism.vi

INTERNATIONAL TOURISM BUREAUS

Anguilla Tourist Information
800-553-4939
www.anguilla-vacation.com

Antigua Tourist Office
212-541-4117
www.antigua-barbuda.org

Argentina Tourist Information
800-722-5737
www.turismo.gov.ar

Aruba Tourism Authority
404-89-ARUBA
www.aruba.com

Australian Tourist Commission
www.australia.com

Austrian National Tourist Office
www.austria-tourism.at

Bahamas Tourist Office
800-422-4262
www.bahamas.com

Balkan Holidays
800-822-1106
www.balkan-travel.com

Barbados Board of Tourism
800-221-9831
www.barbados.org

Belgian Tourist Office
212-758-8130
www.visitbelgium.com

Belize Tourist Board
800-624-0686
travelbelize.org

Bermuda Department of Tourism
800-BERMUDA
www.bermudatourism.com

Bonaire Tourist Information Office
800-BONAIRE
www.infobonaire.com

Brazil Tourism Office
800-544-5503
www.brazilres.com

Visit Britain
800-462-2748
www.travelbritain.org

HELPFUL RESOURCES

Canadian Consulate
613-946-1000
www.travelcanada.ca

Alberta: 800-661-8888
www.travelalberta.com

British Columbia:
800-HELLO-BC
www.hellobc.com

Manitoba:
800-665-0040
www.travelmanitoba.com

New Brunswick:
800-561-0123
www.tourismnewbrunswick.ca

Newfoundland:
800-563-6353
www.gov.nf.ca/tourism/

Nova Scotia:
800-565-0000
www.explorens.com

Ontario:
800-ONTARIO
www.ontariotravel.net

Prince Edward:
800-PEI-PLAY
www.peiplay.com

Quebec:
877-BONJOUR
www.bonjourquebec.com

Saskatchewan:
877-2-ESCAPE
www.sasktourism.com

Yukon:
867-667-5340
www.touryukon.com

Caribbean Tourism Organization
800-603-3545
www.doitcaribbean.com

Cayman Islands Department of Tourism
212-889-9009
www.caymanislands.ky

Chile National Tourist Board
800-244-5366
www.visitchile.com

China National Tourist Office
818-545-7505
www.cnto.org

Colombian Consulate
202-332-7476
www.colombiaemb.org

Cook Islands Tourist Authority
888-994-2665
www.cook-islands.com

Costa Rican Tourist Board
800-343-6332
www.visitcostarica.com

Curacao Tourist Board
800-683-7660
www.curacao-tourism.com

Cyprus Consulate General
212-683-5280
www.cyprustourism.org

**CEDOK
(Czech Republic and Slovakia)**
212-288-0830
www.czechcenter.com

Denmark Tourist Board
212-885-9700
www.visitdenmark.com

Dominican Republic Tourist Info. Center
888-DR-INFO
www.dominica.com.do

Egyptian Tourist Authority
312-280-4666
touregypt.net

Fiji Visitors Bureau
800-YEA-FIJI
www.BulaFiji.com

Finland Tourist Board
800-FIN-INFO
www.gofinland.org

French Government Tourist Office
410-286-8310
www.franceguide.com

French West Indies
877-956-1234

German National Tourist Office
323-655-6085
www.visits-to-germany.com

Greece National Tourist Authority
212-421-5777
www.greektourism.com

Grenada Department of Tourism
212-687-9554
www.grenada.org

Guam Visitors Bureau
800-US-3-GUAM
www.visitguam.org

**Guatemala Tourist
Commission**
888-464-8281
www.guatemala.travel.com.gt

Honduras Tourist Bureau
800-410-9608
www.honduras.com

Hong Kong Tourist Association
212-421-3382
www.discoverhongkong,com/usa/

Hungary Tourist Board
212-355-0240
www.gotohungary.com

Iceland Tourist Board
212-885-9747
www.icetourist.is

India Tourist Office
800-953-9399
www.tourismindia.com

Indonesian Tourist Office
808-638-8500
www.indonesia2001.com

Ireland Tourist Board

800-223-6470
www.tourismireland.com

**Israeli Government
Tourist Office**
888-77-ISRAEL
www.goisrael.com

Italian Tourist Office
212-245-4822
www.italiantourism.com

Jamaican Tourist Board
800-JAMAICA
www.jamaicatravel.com

**Japan National
Tourist Office**
212-757-5640
www.japantravelinfo.com

Kenya Tourist Office
202-387-6101
www.magicalkenya.com

**Korea National
Tourist Office**
800-868-7567
www.tour2korea.com

**Luxembourg National
Tourist Office**
212-935-8888
www.visitluxembourg.com

Macau Tourist Office
www.macautourism.gov.mo

Malaysian Tourist Centre
213-689-9702
www.tourismmalysia.com

Malta National Tourist Office
212-430-3799
www.visitmalta.com

Mexican Tourist Office
800-44-MEXICO
www.visitmexico.com

**Monaco Government
Tourist Office**
800-753-9696
www.visitmonaco.com

Morocco National Tourist Office
wwww.tourism-in-morocco.com

Netherlands Board of Tourism
416-363-1577
www.goholland.com

New Zealand Tourist Office
800-NEW-ZEALAND
www.newzealand.com

**Norway Scandinavia
Tourist Offices**
212-421-7333

www.norway.org

**Papua/New Guinea
Tourist Office**
949-752-5440
www.pngtourism.org.pg

**Philippine Department
of Tourism**
213-487-4525
wowphilippines.com.ph

**Poland National
Tourism Office**
201-420-3370
www.polandtour.org

**Portugal National
Tourist Office**
212-354-4403
www.portugal.org

Puerto Rico Tourism Office
800-866-STAR
www.gotopuertorico.com

**Romanian National
Tourist Office**
212-545-8484
www.romaniatourism.com

**Russian Travel
Information Office**
877-221-7120

www.russia-travel.com

Singapore Tourist Board
323-852-1901
www.singapore-usa.com

South African Tourism Board
800-822-5368
www.satour.org

Spain National Tourism Office
212-265-8822
www.okspain.org

Sri Lanka Tourist Board
202-483-4025
www.slembassyusa.org

St. Kitts Tourist Board
212-535-1234
www.stkittsnevis.org

St. Lucia Tourist Board
800-4-ST-LUCIA
www.stlucia.org

St. Maarten Tourist Office
800-786-2278
www.st-maarten.com

**St. Vincent/Grenadines
Tourist Office**
212-687-4981
www.svgtourism.com

**Sweden Travel &
Tourism Board**
212-885-9700
www.visit-sweden.com

**Switzerland National
Tourist Office**
877-SWITZERLAND
www.myswitzerland.com

Tahitian Tourist Board
310-414-8484
www.tahiti-tourisme.com

Taiwan Visitors Association
212-867-1632
www.taiwan.net.tw

Thailand Tourism Authority
212-432-0433
www.tourismthailand.org

**Trinidad and Tobago
Tourist Board**
www.visitTNT.com

Tunisian Tourist Office
202-862-1850
www.tourismtunisia.com

Turkish Tourism Office
212-687-2194
www.tourismturkey.org

Venezuela Tourism Association
415-331-0100
www.venezuela.com

OTHER TOURISM BUREAUS AND SERVICES

National Park Service
202-208-4747
www.nps.gov

American Automobile Association
407-444-8000
www.aaa.com

Amtrak National Railroad Passenger Info.
800-872-7245
www.amtrak.com

Rail Europe
800-438-7245
www.raileurope.com

Via Rail Canada
800-561-3949
www.viarail.ca

CREATING A
BUDGET

YOU WANT YOUR HONEYMOON to give you luxurious experiences and priceless memories. But you don't want to return from your vacation faced with debts and unnecessary feelings of guilt for not having stayed within a reasonable budget. This should be the vacation of a lifetime. You can make this trip into anything your imagination allows. Pay attention to which experiences or details you would consider a "must have" and prioritize from there.

As you work with your budget, stay focused on those top priority items and allow less "elaborate" solutions for lower priority items. If you stay true to your most important vacation objectives, the minor sacrifices along the way will barely be noticed.

Perhaps, at this point, you don't know how many days your honeymoon will last. Often, the number of days you'll vacation depends on the type of honeymoon you choose.

CREATING A BUDGET

If you (and your travel agent) are designing your own honeymoon, the typical cost-per-day will most likely determine your length of stay. If you opt for a cruise or another type of prearranged vacation, your length of stay will probably be dependent upon the designated length of the travel package. By determining a basic, overall budget at the start, you will know what your limits are. Yes, this is a very romantic time ... but try to remain realistic! Once you have an idea of your spending limits, your choices will be much easier to make.

Don't be discouraged if you're unable to spend an infinite amount of money on this trip. Very few couples are able to live life so carefree. You can still experience a honeymoon that will leave you filled with those priceless memories ... it's all in the planning!

The following budget worksheets will help guide you in creating your honeymoon budget. You may want to make copies of this worksheet so that you can create several budget plans. Keep trying different variations until you are satisfied with how your expenses will be allocated.

When comparing your potential honeymoon options, you'll find that laying out a simple budget is an effective and essential tool for making decisions.

GENERAL BUDGET

Traditionally the groom is responsible for the honeymoon. The groom will take on the challenges of gathering information and working through the necessary details of providing a perfect honeymoon for his new bride ... and himself! Nowadays, many couples find it necessary for both the bride and groom to contribute to the cost in order to experience the honeymoon of their dreams. (Today, the average newlywed couple spends $2,500-$3,500 on their honeymoon.) Many couples, together, determine what each partner will contribute and then shape the budget from there.

Some couples find that including the suggestion of a "Money Contribution Toward a Memorable Honeymoon" as a gift in their bridal registry is a great way for friends and family to contribute to the trip. Some couples also include some version of a "Dollar Dance" at their reception. This is a great way for the bride and groom to dance with many of their guests while accepting the dollar "dance fee" as a contribution to their honeymoon. Some couples choose to pursue less romantic options for building up the honeymoon savings ... part-time jobs, yard sales, etc.

Whatever your methods may be, remember that increasing the amount of money you will spend does not automatically ensure a more pleasurable and enjoyable vacation. Your most important and effective resource is your commitment to planning. You will see that, regardless of what your budget limits may be, your vacation possibilities are endless.

Note: Even if you think you have a good sense of what you will spend (or even if you plan on going with an all-inclusive package) going through this exercise is a smart way to ensure that there will be no surprises later on.

CREATING A BUDGET

GENERAL BUDGET

Amount from the wedding
budget set aside for
the honeymoon: $ _____

Amount groom is able
to contribute from
current funds/savings: $ _____

Amount bride is able
to contribute from
current funds/savings: $ _____

Amount to be saved/acquired $ _____
by groom from now until the
honeymoon date (monthly
contributions, part-time job,
gifts, bonuses):

Amount to be saved/acquired $ _____
by bride from now until the
honeymoon date (monthly
contributions, part-time job,
gifts, bonuses):

General Budget Total Amount:

$ _____

DETAILED BUDGET

BEFORE THE HONEYMOON

Special honeymoon
clothing purchases: $ _____

Bride's trousseau
(honeymoon lingerie): $ _____

Sundries (Helpful Hint: Make a $ _____
list of what you already have and
what you need to purchase. You can
then use these lists as part of your
packing list. See Packing Checklist.):

Film, disposable cameras, $ _____
extra camera batteries:

Maps, guidebooks, $ _____
travel magazines:

Foreign language books $ _____
and tapes, translation
dictionary:

Passport photos, application fees $ _____
(see International Travel):

Medical exam, inoculations $ _____
(see International Travel):

Other items: $ _____

Before the Honeymoon Total Amount:

$ _____

DETAILED BUDGET

DURING THE HONEYMOON

Transportation

Airplane tickets: $ _____

Shuttle or cab
(to and from the airport): $ _____

Car rental, gasoline, tolls: $ _____

Taxis, buses, other public
transportation: $ _____

Transportation Total Amount:

$ _____

Accommodations

Hotel/resort room
(total for entire stay): $ _____

Room service: $ _____

Miscellaneous "hidden costs"
(Phone use, room taxes and
surcharges, chambermaid and
room service tips, in-room
liquor bar and snacks): $ _____

Accommodations Total Amount:

$ _____

DETAILED BUDGET

DURING THE HONEYMOON

Meals

Breakfast:

$ _____ per meal x _____ # of days = $ _____

Lunch:

$ _____ per meal x _____ # of days = $ _____

Casual Dinners:

$ _____ per meal x _____ # of days = $ _____

Formal Dinners:

$ _____ per meal x _____ # of days = $ _____

Picnics, Snacks:

$ _____ per meal x _____ # of days = $ _____

Meals Total Amount:

$ _____

DETAILED BUDGET
DURING THE HONEYMOON

Entertainment

Sport and activity lessons (tennis, golf, ballroom dancing, etc.): $ _____

Day excursions and tours (boat tours, diving, snorkeling, bus/guided tours, etc.): $ _____

Shows, theater: $ _____

Lounges, nightclubs, discos (don't forget to include the cost of drinks and bar gratuities): $ _____

Museum fees: $ _____

Pampering (massages, spa treatments, hairdresser, etc.): $ _____

Entertainment Total Amount:

$ _____

DETAILED BUDGET

DURING THE HONEYMOON

Miscellaneous

Souvenirs for yourselves: $ _____

Souvenirs and gifts for
family and friends: $ _____

Postcards
(including cost of stamps): $ _____

Newspapers and magazines: $ _____

Additional film, replacement $ _____
sundries, other:

Miscellaneous Total Amount:

$ _____

DETAILED BUDGET
AFTER THE HONEYMOON

Film developing costs: $ _____

Photo albums: $ _____

After the Honeymoon Total Amount:

$ _____

For All-Inclusive Resorts/Cruises and Travel Packages Only

Fill in the entire budget form above (simply put a $0.00 on the items to be included in the total package price). Then list the total inclusive package price on the line below. Don't forget to include taxes and surcharges.

Inclusive Package Price: $ _____

Detailed Budget Total Amount:

$ _____

Doing a budget analysis may be one of the most useful things you can do in planning your honeymoon. With all the options available, a good cost analysis will help make the most appropriate decisions very clear to you.

First, create a budget using the previous worksheet for what you think allows for an ideal, yet reasonable, honeymoon. Highlight those expenses which are top priorities. For example, a spacious, ritzy hotel room may be the most important element for you. Or, perhaps participating in numerous sports activities and excursions or enjoying fine dining is more important than a spacious room.

Next, as you come across different destinations and options that appeal to you, fill in a new budget worksheet. Compare the results to other potential trips. See how your priority items on each trip compare to one another. Determine the pros and cons of each. This is also an effective way of looking at the pros and cons of an all-inclusive package versus an independently organized trip.

Note: Once you've decided on your honeymoon destination and activities, fill in a new budget as accurately as possible and take it with you on your trip. Use it to chart your expenses as they occur so you will have a visual guide of whether or not you are staying within budget.

If you find that you are going over your budget, take a look at those top priority items that you'd still like to keep. See if you can eliminate some lower priority items to free up some money for the favored ones.

CREATING A BUDGET

If you find you are under budget, celebrate with a special "gift" for yourselves (massages, an extravagant dinner, another afternoon of jet skiing, etc.).

TIPPING GUIDE

THIS GUIDE IS PROVIDED TO HELP you get familiar with customary gratuity standards you may encounter throughout your travels.

Tipping customs vary from country to country. It is advisable to inquire about tipping with the international tourism board representing the country you'll be traveling in. Simply ask for information about tipping customs and social expectations. You will also want to discuss gratuities with your travel agent or planner. Some travel packages include gratuities in the total cost, some leave that to the guests, and some even discourage tipping (usually because they have built it into the total package price). Be sure to discuss this with your travel planner.

TIPPING GUIDE

SERVICE   **GRATUITY**

AIR TRAVEL

Skycaps .... $1.00 per bag
Flight Attendants .... None

ROAD TRAVEL

Taxi Drivers .... 15% of fare (no less than 50 cents)
Limousine Driver 15%
Valet Parking.. $1.00
Tour Bus Guide $1.00

RAIL TRAVEL

Redcaps........................ $1.00 per bag (or posted rate plus 50 cents)
Sleeping Car Attendant .... $1.00 per person
Train Conductor & Crew .... none
Dining Car Attendant .... 15% of bill

CRUISE

Cabin Steward .... $3 per person per day
Dining Room Waiter..................................... $3 per person per day
Busboy .... $1.50 per person per day
Maitre d'....................At your discretion—recommended $10 - $20
Salon or Spa Personnel... 15%
Bartender .... $1 - $2 per drink

SERVICE	GRATUITY

RESTAURANTS

Maitre d', Head Waiter	None
	(Unless special services provided, then typically $5.00)
Waiter/Waitress	15% of bill (pretax total)
Bartender	$1 - $2 per drink
Wine Steward	15% of bill
Washroom Attendant	$.50 - $1.00
Coat Check Attendant	$1.00 per coat

Note: Some restaurants in foreign countries add the gratuity and/ or service charge to your bill. If it has not been added, tip the customary regional rate.

HOTEL/RESORT

Concierge	$2.00 - $10.00 for special attention or arrangements
Doorman	$1.00 for hailing taxi
Bellhop	$1.00 per bag + $1.00 for showing room
Room Service	15% of bill
Chamber Maid	$1.00 - $2.00 per day or
	$5.00 - $10.00 per week for longer stays
	(no tip for one-night stays)
Pool Attendant	$.50 for towel service

MISCELLANEOUS

Barbershop	15% of cost
Beauty Salon	15% of cost
Manicure	$1.00 - $5.00 depending on cost of service
Facial	15% of cost
Massage	15% of cost

THINGS TO PACK

CONSIDER THE DIFFERENCES IN THE CLIMATES of where you live now and where you'll be visiting. Also consider the air conditions of airplanes, trains and boats. Bring along items that will help in the transition and keep you feeling as comfortable as possible.

TRAVELERS' FIRST AID KIT

- ❐ Aspirin
- ❐ Antacid tablets
- ❐ Diarrhea medication
- ❐ Cold remedies/sinus decongestant
- ❐ Throat lozenges
- ❐ Antiseptic lotion
- ❐ Band-Aids
- ❐ Moleskin for blisters

THINGS TO PACK

- ❒ Breath mints
- ❒ Chapstick
- ❒ Insect repellent, insect bite medication
- ❒ Sunblock and sunburn relief lotion
- ❒ Dry skin lotion/hand cream
- ❒ Eye drops or eye lubricant
- ❒ Saline nasal spray, moisturizing nasal spray
- ❒ Vitamins
- ❒ Prescription drugs

  Note: These should be kept in their original pharmacy containers that provide both drug and doctor information. Be sure to note the drug's generic name. You will want to pack these in your carry-on baggage in case the bags you've checked become lost or delayed.

- ❒ Prescription or other birth control
- ❒ Physicians' names, addresses, and telephone numbers
- ❒ Health insurance phone numbers

  Note: Be sure to contact your provider to find out about coverage while traveling in the U.S. and abroad.

- ❒ Names and phone numbers of people to contact in case of an emergency

PACKING CHECKLIST

CARRY-ON BAGGAGE

❐ Travelers' First Aid Kit (see previous section)
❐ Wallet (credit cards, traveler's checks)
❐ Jewelry and other sentimental and valuable items that you feel you must bring
❐ Identification (passport, driver's license or photo ID)
❐ Photocopies of the following important documents:
❐ Hotel/resort street address, phone number, written confirmation of arrangements and reservations
❐ Complete travel itinerary
❐ Airline tickets
❐ Name, address and phone number of emergency contact person(s) back home
❐ Medicine prescriptions (including generic names) and eyeglass prescription information (or an extra pair); list of food and drug allergies
❐ Phone numbers (including after-hour emergency phone numbers) for health insurance company and personal physicians
❐ Copy of your packing list. This will help you while packing up at the end of your trip. It will also be invaluable if a piece of your luggage gets lost, as you will know the contents that are missing.
❐ List of your traveler's checks' serial numbers and 24-hour phone number for reporting loss or theft

THINGS TO PACK

❏ Phone numbers to the local U.S. embassy or consulate
❏ Any "essential" toiletries and one complete casual outfit in case checked baggage is delayed or lost
❏ Foreign language dictionary or translator
❏ Camera with film loaded
❏ Maps
❏ Small bills/change (in U.S. dollars and in the appropriate foreign currency) for tipping
❏ Currency converter chart or pocket calculator
❏ Reading material
❏ Eyeglasses
❏ Contact lenses
❏ Contact lens cleaner
❏ Sunglasses
❏ Kleenex, gum, breath mints, and any over-the-counter medicine to ease travel discomfort
❏ Inflatable neck pillow (for lengthy travel)
❏ Address book and thank you notes (in case you have lots of traveling time)
❏ This book
❏ Your Budget Sheet

Other items to carry on
   ❏ Other:
   ❏ Other:
   ❏ Other:
   ❏ Other:

CHECKED BAGGAGE

CLOTHING

Casual Wear
Consider the total number of each casual outfit item that you will need.

- ❏ shorts
- ❏ pants
- ❏ tops
- ❏ jackets/sweaters
- ❏ sweatshirts/sweatsuits
- ❏ belts
- ❏ socks
- ❏ underwear/panties & bras
- ❏ walking shoes/sandals/loafers

- ❏ _____
- ❏ _____
- ❏ _____

Athletic Wear
Consider the total number of each sporting outfit item that you will need.

- ❏ shorts
- ❏ sweatpants
- ❏ tops
- ❏ sweatshirts/jackets
- ❏ swimsuits, swimsuit cover-up

THINGS TO PACK

❑ aerobic activity outfit
❑ athletic equipment
❑ socks
❑ underwear/panties & exercise bras
❑ tennis/athletic shoes

❑ _____
❑ _____
❑ _____

Evening Wear
Consider the total number of each evening outfit item that you will need.

❑ pants or pants/skirts/dresses
❑ belts
❑ dress shirts/blouses
❑ sweaters
❑ jackets/blazers/ties
❑ socks or pantyhose/slips
❑ underwear/panties & bras
❑ accessories/jewelry
❑ shoes

❑ _____
❑ _____
❑ _____

Formal Wear
Consider the number of each formal outfit item that you will need.

- ❒ dress pants/suits/tuxedo
- ❒ dresses/gowns
- ❒ accessories/jewelry
- ❒ socks or pantyhose/slips
- ❒ underwear/panties & bras
- ❒ dress shoes

- ❒ _____
- ❒ _____
- ❒ _____

Other clothing items
- ❒ pajamas
- ❒ lingerie
- ❒ slippers
- ❒ robe

- ❒ _____
- ❒ _____
- ❒ _____

MISCELLANEOUS ITEMS

- ❒ An additional set of the important document photo-copies as packed in your carry-on bag
- ❒ Travel tour books, tourism bureau information numbers

THINGS TO PACK

- ❑ Journal
- ❑ Special honeymoon gift for your new spouse
- ❑ Any romantic items or favorite accessories
- ❑ Extra film and camera batteries
- ❑ Plastic bags for dirty laundry
- ❑ Large plastic or nylon tote bag for bringing home new purchases
- ❑ Small sewing kit and safety pins
- ❑ Travel alarm clock
- ❑ Travel iron, lint brush
- ❑ Compact umbrella, fold-up rain slickers
- ❑ Handheld tape recorder (for recorded memory journal or for bringing along your favorite, romantic tapes)
- ❑ Video camera

- ❑ _____
- ❑ _____
- ❑ _____

FOR INTERNATIONAL TRAVEL

- ❑ Passports/visas
- ❑ Electric converters and adapter plugs
- ❑ Copy of appropriate forms showing proof of required vaccinations/inoculations

OTHER ITEMS TO BRING

❐ _____
❐ _____
❐ _____
❐ _____
❐ _____

ITEMS TO LEAVE BEHIND *with a trusted contact person*

❐ Photocopy of all travel details (complete itineraries, names, addresses, and telephone numbers)
❐ Photocopy of credit cards along with 24-hour telephone number to report loss or theft. (Be sure to get the number to call when traveling abroad. It will be a different number than their U.S. 1-800 number.)
❐ Photocopy of traveler's checks along with 24-hour telephone number to report loss or theft
❐ Photocopy of passport identification page, along with date and place of issuance
❐ Photocopy of drivers license
❐ Any irreplaceable items

INTERNATIONAL TRAVEL

THERE ARE OVER 250 U.S. EMBASSIES and consulates around the world. After contacting the Tourism Bureau for the area you will be traveling to, it is also a wise idea to contact the U.S. Embassy or Consulate for that region. With assistance from both of these sources you will be able to determine the travel requirements and recommendations for your chosen travel destination. Within this section you will find numerous resources to assure all of your questions and concerns are addressed before you travel. Call for a list of U.S. embassy and consulate locations with emergency phone numbers: (202) 647-5225 or visit http://travel.state.gov

PASSPORTS AND VISAS

Your travel agent should be able to provide you with information to adequately prepare you for your international travels. Additional information (and possibly more detailed and current information) can be obtained by contacting the appropriate sources listed in this section.

As a U.S. citizen, you generally need a passport to enter and to depart most foreign countries and to reenter the United States. Some countries also require visas. A visa is an endorsement by officials of a foreign country as permission to visit their country. You first need a passport in order to obtain a visa. Inquire with the resources listed in this section for requirements of your specific destination.

As mentioned, you will be required to prove your U.S. citizenship upon reentry to the United States. If the country of your destination does not require you to possess a current passport, you will still need to produce proof of citizenship for U.S. Immigration. Items that are acceptable as proof of citizenship include a passport, a certified copy of your birth certificate, Certificate of Nationalization, a Certificate of Citizenship, or a Report of Birth Abroad of a Citizen of the United States. Proof of identification can include a driver's license or a government or military identification card containing a photo or physical description.

Note: The bride should have her passport and airline tickets reflect her maiden name for ease in proof of identification while traveling. Name changes can be processed after returning from the honeymoon with your marriage certificate.

Your passport will be one of the most important documents you will take with you. Contact the local U.S. Embassy immediately if your passport becomes lost or stolen. Have